Welcome to

iPad
for Beginners

A6X chip
with retina display
16 GB

The iPad is one of the most intriguing products to have been released in recent times. Allowing you to have extreme portability while still being able to do an incredible amount of day-to-day tasks, the iPad 2 and third-generation iPad, in particular, act as a camera, movable media hub, games console and much more, all alongside one of the most user-friendly and dynamic interfaces. It potentially changes the way we have being going about our lives for the last few years. The recent release of iOS 6 has seen further additions and improvements to apps such as Maps, Facebook and Siri, as well as the iPad's core apps such as Mail and Safari. So now you have your eager hands on this revolutionary device, **iPad for Beginners** will help you find your way around it. From downloading apps and syncing with iCloud, all the way to word processing and taking photos, discover everything you need to know to set up and get started.

iPad
for Beginners™

Imagine Publishing Ltd
Richmond House
33 Richmond Hill
Bournemouth
Dorset BH2 6EZ
☎ +44 (0) 1202 586200
Website: www.imagine-publishing.co.uk
Twitter: @Books_Imagine
Facebook: www.facebook.com/ImagineBookazines

Head of Publishing
Aaron Asadi

Head of Design
Ross Andrews

Production Editor
Sarah Harrison

Senior Art Editor
Danielle Dixon

Design
Rachel Shemilt

Printed by
William Gibbons, 26 Planetary Road, Willenhall, West Midlands, WV13 3XT

Distributed in the UK & Eire by
Imagine Publishing Ltd, www.imagineshop.co.uk. Tel 01202 586200

Distributed in Australia by
Gordon & Gotch, Equinox Centre, 18 Rodborough Road, Frenchs Forest,
NSW 2086. Tel + 61 2 9972 8800

Distributed in the Rest of the World by
Marketforce, Blue Fin Building, 110 Southwark Street, London, SE1 0SU.

Part of the
iCreate™
bookazine series

IMAGINEER OF THE YEAR
DANIELLE DIXON

ip
IMAGINE
PUBLISHING

TEAM OF THE YEAR
BOOKAZINES

Contents

Introduction

Setting up

Getting started

Find your way around the iPad hardware on page 8

150 Feature

100 essential apps

The must-have apps you simply have to download today

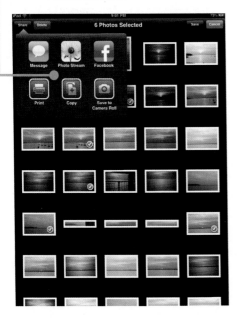

Introduction

Wi-Fi signal strength
This symbol lets you know the signal strength it is receiving

Available with or without 3G
If you want to use your iPad away from a Wi-Fi signal, you'll need the 3G model

16, 32 or 64GB
The iPad comes in various storage sizes – the 16GB is cheapest

The cameras
The iPad has a FaceTime camera on the front and an iSight camera on the back

First look at the iPad

Let's explore the iPad's basic features

The iPad is unlike any computer you've ever laid your hands on. For one thing, there's no intermediary between you and what you're trying to do; on a regular computer, you have to learn to manipulate a pointing device like a mouse or trackpad to move a cursor on the screen so you can achieve what you need to do. On the iPad, you're already an expert manipulator since you just use your fingers directly on the screen to move and affect what you see. If you know how to point, you know how to use an iPad, and that's the truly

exciting thing about this device: it makes personal computing truly personal.

But despite its obvious friendliness, it's still a remarkably complex piece of hardware and you'll need to know a little about what makes the iPad tick: how you turn it on, for instance, and what functions its few buttons offer. And what about all the other controls embedded in the software itself? How can you use its many features to the fullest?

We will endeavour to show you all this over the next few pages, helping you feel comfortable with the device so you can hit the ground running in no time at all.

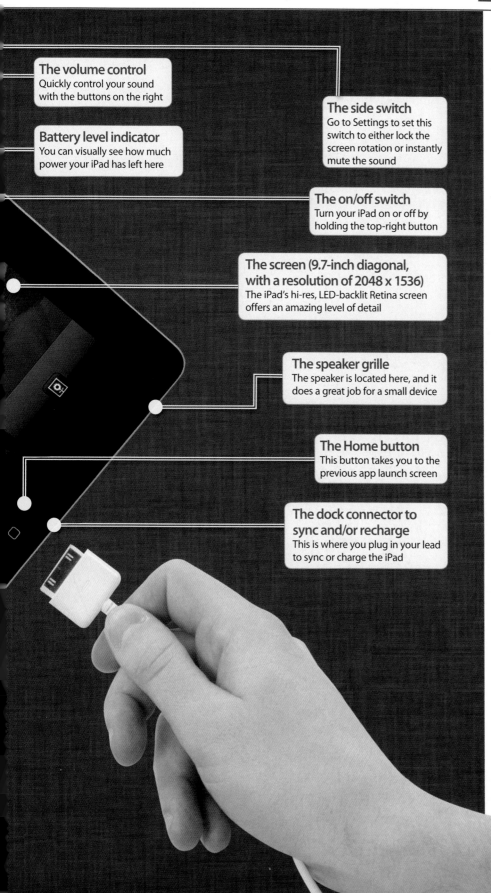

The volume control
Quickly control your sound with the buttons on the right

Battery level indicator
You can visually see how much power your iPad has left here

The side switch
Go to Settings to set this switch to either lock the screen rotation or instantly mute the sound

The on/off switch
Turn your iPad on or off by holding the top-right button

The screen (9.7-inch diagonal, with a resolution of 2048 x 1536)
The iPad's hi-res, LED-backlit Retina screen offers an amazing level of detail

The speaker grille
The speaker is located here, and it does a great job for a small device

The Home button
This button takes you to the previous app launch screen

The dock connector to sync and/or recharge
This is where you plug in your lead to sync or charge the iPad

Browsing

As soon as you've connected to your local wireless network, the iPad is ready to be an internet browsing device. In fact, when Apple's engineers were first experimenting with touch-screen devices, the original idea was a tablet designed for web browsing. As a result, going online is a very polished experience and a joy to use. Like all other applications on the iPad, tapping on the Safari icon fills the screen with that program's content, removing any other distractions from view. You can then browse the web with your fingers. If you're familiar with Safari on your Mac or PC, you'll feel right at home – there's even a Google search field, top right of the screen. Tapping on it increases its size and reveals the keyboard so you can type what you're looking for. The same applies for the address field if you know exactly where you want to go.

Thanks to iCloud, you can sync your Mac's bookmarks straight to your iPad, right down to the Bookmark Bar.

Navigating a webpage is easy: you flick your finger up, down, left or right to see other parts of the page. If you want to focus on a specific section, double-tap on it to zoom in on it.

There are other browsers on the App Store, such as Opera Mini and Atomic, so have a look to see if one suits your needs better than Safari.

Communication

Browsing the web isn't the only thing you need to do online. For one thing, you need to check your emails and the iPad's got you covered there as well, thanks to the Mail application. With it, you can set up as many accounts as you need. Just like Mail on your Mac, you have a universal inbox where all your messages, irrespective of which address they were sent to, can be accessed, read and replied to. You can also organise your messages in threads, making it easier to keep track of a conversation over time.

When it comes to social networking, you can either make use of Safari – aside from its games, Facebook works very well in the iPad's web browser (the games don't work because they rely on

Introduction

Adobe's Flash platform, which isn't compatible with the iPad, iPhone or iPod touch) – or look for the dedicated iPad apps, like Facebook and Twitter, at the App Store. The latter has even been integrated into iOS 6 so that you can tweet from within a host of default Apple apps.

Other applications, like Skype, are also available, meaning you can enjoy full-screen video calls on your iPad with other people who don't necessarily own an Apple device, or there's the default FaceTime app for people who do.

Photos

If you see images on the web you'd like to keep, you can easily save them to your Photos application by tapping and holding on one and choosing 'Save Image' from the popover menu. But that's not the only use of that particular program. Thanks to iOS 6's iCloud feature, you can activate Photo Stream so that any pictures taken on your iPad or iPhone are automatically pushed to all of your iOS 6 devices and Macs running OS X 10.7.2 or higher.

You can also dispense with a bigger computer entirely by getting the iPad Camera Connection Kit and transfer photos and videos from any compatible digital stills camera straight to your iPad library – after which Photo Stream will make them instantly available on all of your devices, automatically and completely wirelessly.

Once there, you can browse through your photos, post them online or send them via email to friends and family. If you want to upload them to Facebook or Twitter, you can do this via the Photo app. Select the image you want to use and tap the Share button to see the options. You can also set it as wallpaper.

First steps

Getting acquainted with your iPad

Turn on
When an iPad's screen is off, your device is either asleep or shut down

01 To turn the device on when it has been fully turned off, press the on/off button, top right of the device.

02 If it's in Sleep mode, you can also press the Home button to bring your iPad back to life.

Sleep mode
Putting your iPad to sleep is something you'll find yourself doing quite often

01 You need to make use of one of your iPad's few physical buttons for this,: the on/off one, top right of the device.

02 Press and release it once for the screen to go dark and become unresponsive to any touch input.

Turn off
Most of the time, you'll keep the iPad on but asleep. To shut down, do the following

01 Press and hold on its on/off button for up to five seconds. The screen will dim and a red slider will appear.

02 Move that red slider from left to right to confirm that you wish to shut the iPad down.

Change volume
Depending on what you're doing, you can change the volume in various ways

01 Use the physical buttons, top of the iPad's right edge. The top one increases the volume and the bottom one lowers it.

02 If you're watching a movie or listening to music, you'll find a slider on the screen to achieve the same result.

Rotation lock
You may wish to stop the screen from rotating each time you change position. Here's how

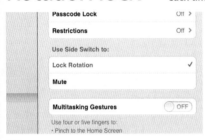

01 Go to Settings and, under General there, set the 'Use Side Switch to:' option to Lock Rotation and then slide the side switch.

02 If your side switch is set to Mute, double-tap the Home button, scroll to the right and then tap the lock button.

Brightness
If the screen is too light or dark for your tastes, you can alter it in a couple of ways

01 Tap on the Settings app and select the 'Brightness & Wallpaper' menu. Use the slider to lower or raise the brightness.

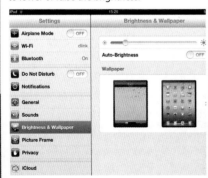

02 Double-click the Home button and slide the new bar of icons to the right. You'll find a brightness slider there as well.

Unlock
Once you've woken your iPad up, you'll be graced with its Lock Screen. What next?

01 To gain access to your device, use the slider at the bottom to unlock your screen.

02 If you have set a password, you will have to type it in before you can proceed any further.

Mute
To mute the volume, you have two options based on the iPad's physical buttons

01 If you have the side switch set to Mute, slide it down to mute your iPad.

02 You can also press and hold the volume-down button. After a couple of seconds, your iPad will be muted.

Charge
Recharging the iPad is a simple matter

01 Unless your computer is recent enough, there won't be enough power from its USB port to charge the iPad.

02 For a faster, more efficient charge, it's best to use the bundled power adaptor instead.

Sync
To back up or transfer files, you need to sync

01 Use the bundled cable to connect your iPad via one of your computer's USB ports.

Sync with iCloud Go to page 30 for this syncing option

02 It will launch iTunes and the backup and syncing process will by default be totally automatic.

Introduction

"From the Music app, you gain access to your songs, podcasts and audiobooks"

Music

It wouldn't be an Apple device if it didn't let you listen to your music, but although iTunes is responsible for almost everything media-related on your Mac, the iPad has broken those features into multiple applications designed for specific purposes. For instance, you can purchase new music using the iTunes application, but if you want to listen to albums you currently own, then you have to use the Music app. From there, you gain access to your songs, podcasts and audiobooks. If you want to watch a music video, however, you'll need to take a trip to the Videos application.

But iTunes isn't the only way you can listen to music on your iPad. There are other programs that let you stream songs directly from the internet and, just like the Music application, they can be used to listen to music in the background while you work in another program on your iPad. If you're in the UK, make sure you check out Spotify, while US readers should take a look at Pandora.

Watching

Although it's no substitute for your widescreen television, when you're away from your couch, the iPad makes for a surprisingly good TV. Due to its size, it's much better than an iPhone or iPod touch and its built-in speaker is good enough to allow the device to be shared, but what can you watch on it? Well, anything you've bought or rented from the iTunes Store will work on your iPad: you can transfer movies, TV shows, podcasts and music videos and they'll all play flawlessly on your portable device.

"Videos all play flawlessly on your portable device"

You could also convert your existing DVD collection into iTunes-compatible files; but in order to achieve this, you'd need programs like HandBrake which are designed to transform your films and episodes into compatible files ready for you to enjoy on your iPad. This can be a time-consuming process, so why not try the brilliant television services such as the BBC iPlayer and Sky Go, both of which offer catch-up services? The Sky+ app lets UK viewers record programmes remotely to watch on their Sky+ in-home boxes. The EyeTV application also lets you watch live TV as long as you're within range of your wireless signal.

Entertainment

There's been a lot of talk about the iPad (and other iOS devices) not being compatible with Adobe's Flash, but this is actually less of a problem than you might think. For one thing, although you won't be able to go to www.youtube.com and watch videos via the Safari web browser, there's a dedicated YouTube application which enables you to do just that. You can watch clips, comment on them and do pretty much everything you'd expect, but you will need to download this from the App Store since Apple removed the built-in YouTube app from iOS 6. Other video-sharing sites, like Vimeo, offer iPad-compatible versions of their videos, so you can watch those straight from your web browser.

But being entertained is much more than just passively watching something on the screen; you can also use your iPad to read the latest bestseller or enjoy a timeless classic. The two major programs that allow you to do this are Apple's own iBooks and Amazon's Kindle. Both are also compatible with the iPod and iPhone, so you can stop reading on the iPad and carry on with another device if you'd like. That compatibility doesn't extend to your Mac for the iBooks, but it does for the Kindle. Not all titles are available in digital form yet, but there's enough there to keep you busy for a long time.

Games

When it comes to games, you'll be spoilt for choice. There are so many available to download, both free and paid-for. You can spend hours getting immersed in an adventure story (thank goodness for the iPad's excellent battery life), or just use it to while away a few minutes of your time.

The obvious choices are there, like arcade-style games such as *The Incident* and *Fruit Ninja HD*; plus adventure games like *Hero of Sparta 2* and *Max*; strategy games like *Cut the Rope* and *Angry Birds*; and role-playing games like *Aralon* and *Galaxy on Fire 2*. There's even a version of *Farmville*.

But none of these offers anything new from what you could achieve on a regular computer. What sets the iPad apart from other platforms is that its screen is large enough that it can be easily viewed by multiple people at the same time. As a result, it's become a natural digital alternative to board games, making playing on a computer a much more social experience with people in the same room as you, just like the good old days. Make sure you check out titles like *WarChess*, *Carcassonne*, *Scrabble*, *Monopoly* and *The Game Of Life*. Whatever your tastes, though, the iPad has it covered.

iTunes
The desktop software explored

What is iTunes?
It's a program designed by Apple and the original purpose was to transfer your CD collection onto your Mac, catalogue your songs and transfer them to a compatible MP3 player. A lot's changed since those humble days.

Why do I need it?
Because iTunes evolved over the years to accommodate more than music – movies, TV shows, podcasts and more. Now it's the most popular way to transfer anything to your iPad.

Why is it not included on a CD?
Apple now assumes that broadband is ubiquitous, and that way the company can make sure that you'll be using the very latest version available as opposed to one that could have been released months previously.

How do I cancel the sync?
When your iPad is connected to iTunes, its screen informs you not to disconnect it from your computer. However, there is a slider at the bottom which you can use to cancel the sync should you need to. Note that your iPad will not be fully backed up if you do this, however.

Is there anything else I need to do?
Not really. The syncing process is completely automatic and if you don't want to get any more involved in it, you don't have to. Once the sync is complete, you can unplug your device and carry on using it.

Can I control what's on my iPad?
Absolutely. Look down iTunes's sidebar until you find the Devices section. Click on your iPad and the main part of the interface will let you choose which songs,

Where can I get it?

Point your browser towards www.itunes.com and click on the 'Download iTunes' button, somewhere on the page (it's currently on the right, near the top, but that could change).

It's installed. Now what?
Double-click on its icon to open it and agree to the licence agreement. You can convert your music CDs to iPad-compatible files or purchase new songs, movies and shows from the iTunes Store. But none of this is compulsory.

What happens when I connect my iPad to my computer?
iTunes will take over your iPad and you will be asked not to disconnect it while the syncing process is taking place. Your iPad's data will be backed up and your media will be synchronised between both of your devices.

films, podcasts, applications and so on you'd like to transfer over.

What about my emails, calendars and contacts?
That's all possible to sync as well, from the same section in iTunes as mentioned above. You can find all the details and choose which calendars, contacts and emails you'd like to import from the Info section.

Introduction

"Chances are someone may already have designed a great solution that fits your exact needs"

Office work

The iPad isn't just a device to browse the web, watch videos and play games, however. Many people classify it as just a media consumption device, but it's in fact a very powerful machine capable of doing almost anything a regular computer can. It comes with a Notes program which you can use to jot down a few ideas, lists or even the beginning of a draft letter. That application syncs with your emails and you can access those documents in your Mac's Mail program, which is very convenient and enables you to work between the two systems.

But the iPad can go a lot further than this. For one thing, the iWork suite is available for it as a separate purchase. You obviously won't get all the features you've grown accustomed to with the Mac's versions, but for a first attempt at creating a business suite that's controlled by touch, it's remarkable what you can do with these apps and you'll be designing newsletters, filling in spreadsheets and creating presentations in next to no time.

If you need compatibility with Microsoft Word and iWork's conversion layer isn't good enough, take a look at Byte²'s Office² HD. It's not as attractive as the iWork suite, but it lets you create native Word (both .doc and .docx) and Excel (.xls) documents on your iPad for a very reasonable price.

Productivity

As for other productivity programs, Calendar stores all your appointments and syncs with Calendar on your Mac – as long as you have activated your free iOS 6 iCloud account. The same applies for the Contacts app, even preserving all your groups so you'll feel right at home on your new machine.

Surprisingly, unlike the iPod touch or iPhone, the iPad doesn't come with a calculator, but this can be easily remedied with a short visit to the App Store. Just type in "Calculator" in the search field to find enough free and paid options to satisfy your needs.

Another feature missing from the iPad is any possibility of using it like an external drive, but the fantastic advantage of the iPad (and any device powered by the iOS software) is the huge number of developers working on it. As a result, someone's come up with a way of achieving just that, thanks to an application called 'USB Disk Pro for iPad' (a free version is also available under the title of 'USB Disk for iPad'), so you can easily use your iPad like an external portable hard drive.

Chances are, whatever it is you're looking for, someone may already have designed a solution that fits your exact needs.

Creative apps

That's exactly the case with graphic design applications. Adobe, maker of the mighty Photoshop, has only dipped its toes into the iPad, but other, smaller developers have jumped at the opportunity that this new platform offers them and there's a wealth of programs that allow you to design with your fingers anything you used to need a mouse or a graphic tablet for in the past.

App Store

A vital part of the iPad explained

What's all this talk about apps? Do I need them?

Apps, or applications, are programs that run on a computer, like your browser or word processor. They increase your device's functionality and you should definitely browse through them to see if there's anything you might find crucial to your life on the iPad. You'll be glad you did.

Where do I get these apps?

Straight from the App Store, which you can access from iTunes or the iPad app. You might find some websites showcasing various programs, but you can only get them from the App Store.

What if I'm just browsing? Can I find stuff easily?

Of course: the App Store is really designed to help you buy programs. As a result, you can look through various lists like top sellers, top free apps, staff recommendations, and so on.

Is there any trial software I can use?

Not as such, but many developers have 'lite' or 'free' versions of their applications. These offer limited functionality or a few sample levels if it's a game. If you like what you see, you can then purchase the full program and delete the lite copy.

How do I find what I want?

With over 60,000 apps designed specifically for the iPad, you may feel that you may never find the exact program you need. Try using the search field to narrow down the results.

Can I only get them from my computer?

No: there's a program called 'App Store' on your iPad. From there, you can gain access to the entire store as well, although you will need to be within range of a Wi-Fi network, unless of course you own a 3G-capable iPad.

It's all a bit of a jumble; can I narrow my search down?

The App Store is broken into 20 categories, each with its own top sellers list. You can narrow your search by focusing on a single category.

Why can't I comment on a program I'm looking at?

In order to limit bogus reviews or overly negative or positive comments from people who've never used the program, Apple links your reviews to your account. The company can therefore check if you own the app and if you do not, you can only read, not contribute.

How can I ask questions or get help from the developer?

At the bottom of every app description is a link to the developer's own website. More often than not, you'll find a help forum or contact email address there, which you can use to write to the developer or company and get the help you need.

Why does my App Store icon have red numbers on it?

These badges are there to show you that some of the programs you've acquired have been updated and that you can get those new versions for free directly from the App Store's Updates section on your iPad (or computer).

"The iPad is a very powerful machine capable of doing almost anything a computer can"

The beauty of the iPad is that these programs are so cheap compared to those you'd find on a Mac or PC that trying some out isn't as financially crippling as it can be on other platforms.

You're bound to find the right program that matches your abilities. If you're artistically inclined, have a look at SketchBook Pro, Freeform or Brushes. If you're looking for programs that help you transform pictures into visually stunning works of art, explore Artist's Touch or the PhotoArtistaHD series of applications. If you fancy more specific effects, consider TypeDrawing or Glow Painter Pro HD. Those of you missing iPhoto's adjustment tools should purchase TouchUp, and your children (or the child inside you) will love Drawing Pad.

Introduction

Kids

The iPad is an amazing learning tool no matter what your age is; there's even a dedicated section called 'Apps for Kids' in the App Store, where you can get interactive books like *Winnie the Pooh* or *The Cat in the Hat*, programs that teach you how to read and write or even understand the world around you, help you play music, draw… pretty much anything you can imagine.

Older children haven't been left out either: MathBoard is a fantastic program designed to help you perfect your algebra. You can even set which calculations to work on and how difficult they should be. There are also things to keep kids entertained, such as wordsearch apps like WordSeek HD and much more.

If you're interested in space, you can learn everything you need to know thanks to programs like Solar Walk or Solar System for iPad, and the little ones can keep up with their older siblings with iLearn Solar System HD. If it's dinosaurs you're after, check out Ultimate Dinopedia, and if you want to explore all the elements that make up our universe, be sure to look for The Elements – there's even a British edition with UK English spelling.

Maps

All of the above can be achieved whether you own a Wi-Fi-only iPad or one capable of connecting to a 3G network (ie one that hooks up to a mobile phone network and hence gets you online wherever you have coverage – for a price). If you've decided to invest in a 3G-capable iPad, the capabilities of your machine are greatly extended since you'll be able to browse, check you emails or even play online games wherever you might be.

There's also the added advantage of being able to use the Maps application to help you navigate to your desired location. Apple replaced the Google Maps app with its own for iOS 6, but it does give turn-by-turn directions and hooks into the Siri function too. You may get tired of hearing how 'magical' the iPad is, but it's undeniable how truly amazing it is to be able to scroll through a map and effortlessly zoom in and out of a location using your fingers alone. The program is incredibly responsive and the only limitation you'll experience will be due to your internet's bandwidth. It illustrates just how wonderful using this device truly is. There are also other map apps available, so check out the App Store to find one that suits you.

Accessories

Enrich your hardware with some great kit…

Keyboard The iPad is great for many things, although some people still struggle with typing using the device. You can get around this by purchasing an Apple Wireless Keyboard and then pairing it with your iPad via Bluetooth

Smartcase This device will enthral you for hours with its ingenuity. With the clever use of magnets, you can, literally, sling this cover at your iPad and it will auto-align to sit perfectly across the screen of your device for supreme protection. What's more, when you pull it back, your device will automatically wake up

Case Getting an iPad case is essential if you wish to protect your investment and they come in many styles. Most can display your iPad in portrait or landscape orientation and can be supported at a variety of angles for browsing, working or watching movies

Speakers The iPad's mono speaker may be surprisingly good for an item of its size, but it's really not sufficient to enjoy your media to the fullest. Thankfully, there are many external speakers available to improve the experience. They either connect via its mini-jack, the dock connector or even wirelessly via Bluetooth

Protective films
Even if you prefer your iPad to be without a case, you should consider a film to protect its most important part: the screen. Some high-quality ones not only protect it from accidental scratches, they actually make it easier to clean and fingerprints don't stick as easily as they would on a bare piece of glass

Apple TV Your iPad is a great device to play all of your downloaded movies, videos and music, but if you want to broadcast them on a bigger stage then Apple TV is perfect. This device transforms your TV into a viewing portal for all of your Apple content and it does so wirelessly – you just sit back and control your evening's entertainment from your iPad

Styluses Controlling objects with your fingers undoubtedly feels more natural, but a stylus can be great for precision work. A few companies have created such devices that work very well with the iPad's capacitive screen

Feature

The complete guide to iOS 6

Everything you need to know about Apple's new mobile operating system

iOS 5 had been out for just a few months when Apple announced the next version of its operating system for iPhone, iPod touch and iPad. When it unveiled the new iOS 6 at its Worldwide Developer Conference, there was a whole range of new features that users never even knew they needed. Many of these had been re-evaluated by the Cupertino company. The move to cloud computing is gathering serious speed, as can be seen in the new iCloud Tabs feature in Safari.

Other new standout features include a complete overhaul of the App Store. There are plenty of things to look forward to including a lot of new options for Siri, now available on the new iPad, along with a Maps app that's been rebuilt from the ground up.

iOS 6 is a huge update and, thanks to the system added in iOS 5, the new version can be downloaded for free without connecting up to your computer. This is called an over-the-air update and it makes getting hold of iOS 6 even easier.

Sadly, iOS 6 won't run on every device; it's compatible with the iPhone 3GS, 4, 4S and 5, the fourth-generation iPod touch, the iPad 2 and the newest iPad model. Those using older devices will be disappointed, as they won't be able to enjoy the newest features of iOS 6. However, if you have a compatible iPad you can look forward to some of the biggest updates the device has seen, and make the most of some fantastic new features that ensure your tablet is the best it can be.

The best Maps yet

Since the iPad's launch, iOS has used Google Maps as the basis for its mapping capabilities. Now Apple has had enough of that partnership and has built its own platform from the ground up. The new Maps is vector-based, meaning that as you zoom in everything stays smooth and incredibly detailed. Plus, unlike Google's mapping platform for iOS, you can pinch and twist to rotate the map around.

The app also features turn-by-turn navigation, enabling you to use your iOS device like a satnav. If you're using a Siri-capable device you can speak to your tablet to find new directions and hear Siri tell you where to go next. The newly designed maps are beautiful, too, with a hand-drawn feel that is really unique.

However, for those times that you want a real-life view of a city, there's the brilliant new Flyover feature. Apple has flown planes around major cities of the world and taken aerial photographs from every angle.

Flyover might seem a little dubious as far as feature names are concerned, but it simply refers to the incredible 3D mapping technology that Apple has included with the new Maps app. Combining 3D renders of cityscapes, skinned with satellite imagery of real places, Flyover provides one of the most immersive mapping experiences we've ever seen.

The new Maps app is the biggest update in iOS 6 and one we can't wait to tell you more about.

"The app also features turn-by-turn navigation"

Talk more with Siri in iOS 6

Siri was introduced on the iPhone 4S and it's been vastly improved in iOS 6. Now also available on the new iPad, Siri has seen numerous improvements. For a start it understands a lot more languages, including Korean and Mandarin. However, one of the biggest updates is the fact that local search has gone worldwide. Now you can ask Siri to look things up in your local area no matter where you are in the world, something that will be welcomed by many people.

Siri has learnt a lot more in the last year, too. It can now answer questions about all your favourite sports, from football to basketball. Whether you want game schedules, scores or information about the players, your personal assistant can help whenever it's called upon, keeping you right up to date at all times.

It also knows all about films and lets you book tickets with just a few words. You can ask about nearby restaurants, book tables and read reviews. You can even launch apps with your voice alone and at long last tweet and send Facebook updates with just a few spoken words. This latest update really makes the most of Siri, meaning that something many people were wary of will soon become one of their favourite features.

"You can even launch apps with your voice alone"

Share photos with Photo Stream

Since iCloud launched well over a year ago, users have been able to use Photo Stream, a method that automatically backs up photos to the cloud. This backup lasts for 1,000 photos or 30 days, enabling you to safely store all your latest snaps without even thinking about it.

In iOS 6, you finally have the ability to share the shots you send to Photo Stream. Simply select the photos you want to share and you can create an album to send to your friends and family.

They will be notified that there are newly shared photos and can then flick through what you've shared on their own Apple devices. If they don't own a Mac, an iPhone or an iPad, they can access the photos through a specially designed website, which displays your shots in a beautifully presented grid. Then users can Like or comment on their favourite shots and everyone who is sharing the album will see what they have said. It's another great-looking feature that we can't wait to try out.

This is a huge step forward for Photo Stream and offers yet another sharing option for your photos in iOS 6. Far from being an overlooked feature of the Photos app, this will bring Photo Stream to the fore.

"Apple has built Facebook sharing right in to the new iOS"

Share with friends, from anywhere

In iOS 6 it's even easier to share with friends and family, no matter what you're doing on your iPad. Whether you want to send a status update to your Timeline, or just wish to share a photo, website or Game Center high score, you can do so in a flash with just a few simple taps of the screen.

Much like the Twitter integration that was included in iOS 5 in 2011, Apple has built Facebook sharing right in to the new iOS. When you're viewing photos in your Photos app or iPhoto, the Sharing button will now show a new design, with Facebook at the centre. Details can also be pulled from your friends' profiles and saved to your own Contacts app. Birthdays and other upcoming events will be added to your calendar automatically. Also, with the newly redesigned App Store, you can Like apps directly, as well as see which of your friends Like particular apps you're viewing. So how do you go about getting all these features? Simply sign in once and your device will remember you automatically. If you're a heavy Facebook user, this latest update will make your life a whole lot easier.

Smarter browsing with iOS 6 Safari

Safari has been at the core of iOS since its launch in 2007, and it's been getting regular updates since. The new version of iOS brings a ream of new features to match some of the characteristics from its brothers on Mac and PC.

iCloud Tabs, for example, enables you to see a list of all the tabs you currently have open on other devices. This means that if you lock your iPad with three tabs open in Safari, you can quickly and easily access them on your iPhone with a few taps and pick up where you left off.

The iOS 6 update also features Offline Reading List, which enables you to save online articles for reading later. You can even view your saved articles without a connection to the internet, because they are automatically saved to your iPad's internal memory. It's yet another move to ensure iOS is the most user-friendly operating system. These are small updates, but they will change how we browse on our devices forever.

"The new Guided Access feature enables users to restrict certain features of the device"

iOS for everyone

One of Apple's biggest focuses when it makes iOS devices is on accessibility. Over the last few years it has pushed hard to ensure that everyone can use iPads and iPhones easily, including those with vision, hearing, learning and mobility issues. Before, there were a few useful features that helped everyone use the iPad and iPhone, but in iOS 6 Apple has taken it a step further.

The new Guided Access feature enables users to restrict certain features of the device in specific apps. For teachers or parents it's perfect, as it means both young kids and those with disabilities can use the device without frustration. Switching off the functions of the Home button, for example, will stop people exiting the app accidentally. You can also circle areas on-screen and inside these areas touches won't be recognised.

Of course, you don't have to enable Guided Access and by default its settings will all be turned off. To see what they can do, enter Settings and search for the Accessibility option.

Video chat anywhere with FaceTime

While FaceTime is a brilliant way to catch up with friends, it's been slightly limited by the fact that it was only possible to call people when connected to a wireless network. Now, with iOS 6, it's possible to make a FaceTime call using your iPad (with 3 or 4G) anywhere. This is thanks to the fact that it has now been enabled over mobile networks as well as local Wi-Fi networks.

This means that no matter where you are in the world, if you have a good enough signal you'll be able to chat to anyone and see their face at the same time. Plus, with the addition of 4G on the latest iPad, your calls won't ever need to suffer from stuttering or disconnections, with the fastest speeds available everywhere. This means the people you can reach when calling from your tablet will certainly increase. Also, iOS 6 enables you to link your Apple ID and phone number, so even if friends call you using a phone number, you can answer the call on your iPad.

Stay in touch with Mail

When Apple carried out a survey last year, it found that one of the most regular things that people used their iPads for was sending and reading emails, and with good reason. Tapping out emails on the iPad is fast and fun thanks to the multi-touch interface, while reading your messages with images shown in-line with the text is a beautiful experience.

In iOS 6 there aren't a huge number of changes to the app, as there isn't much more that it needs to do. However, Apple has simply streamlined the interface and made everything even easier.

First, you can make your most important friends and family members VIPs in your Contacts app. A smart mailbox will then automatically separate them from the rest of your emails so you can focus on what is most important to you. Refreshing your mailbox is easier than ever too, rather than tapping a button you now only need to drag the list of messages down to refresh a mailbox.

Finally, adding photos and videos to an email is much easier, with just a few taps. Apple's Mail app on iOS was already a great application, but with these handy updates, it's got a whole lot better.

"Apple has simply streamlined the interface and made everything even easier"

"The improved functionality and usability of the App Store certainly improve the overall experience"

What's in Store?

While Apple's Stores are at the forefront of the iOS experience, little has changed since they launched back in 2008. Now, though, the three stores, for music, apps and books have received a much-welcome overhaul to provide users with a new seamless shopping experience. You'll be able to see the best of new content in each store's Homepage, browse items by swiping your fingers and share your favourite apps through Facebook and Twitter. The whole process is more user-friendly and intuitive than it has ever been before.

App developers also have the ability to link to their apps in an unobtrusive way when you're viewing their website. If, for example, you're shopping on Amazon, a pop-up will appear enabling you to buy the app. If you tap this, you'll be taken to the store to download it, or if you already have it the touch will open it, taking you to the exact page you were viewing.

All stores now have improved iCloud integration, with past purchases available to download to different devices. Genius tabs also provide a personal shopper experience.

It may take a little while to get used to the new-look stores, but the improved functionality and usability certainly improve the overall experience. Finding what you're looking for is now even easier than ever, and before long you'll wonder how you ever managed to use the old, clunky versions of these essential Apple products.

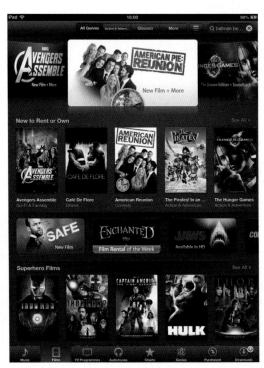

Setting up

Bring your iPad to life with these easy-to-follow tips to get you up and running

"You can now back up all your important iPad data to your own virtual hard drive with iCloud – it's never been easier"

28 Sign in to get started

30 Sync apps with iCloud

35 Copy movies

39 Sync your photos

"Finding your way around the App Store is straightforward – you'll have the best apps in no time"

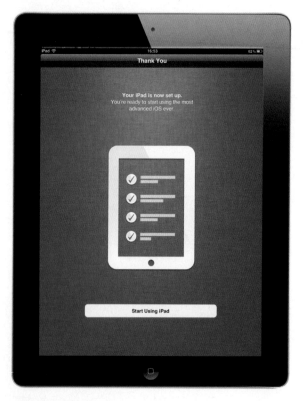

App used: N/A

Time needed: 15 minutes

Activate and register your new iPad

Just got an iPad? We guide you through the process of setting up your device and registering it to your Apple ID

With trembling hands and a giddy sensation in your stomach, you unpack your brand-new iPad from its box and are ready to activate it and start using it to enhance your life. But whereas previously you would have to have had a computer to plug your iPad into to start the setup process, with iOS 5 and iOS 6 you no longer need to tether your device to a computer and the entire setup can be carried out independently, which makes it a quick and easy process.

All you have to do is connect your new device to a power source and then press the Sleep/Wake button, which is situated on the top of your iPad. This will bring up a generic iPad lock screen with a slider at the bottom. Tap and hold on the slider with your index finger and swipe it to the right to unlock the device and the next series of screens will guide you through the setup process. In this tutorial we will take you through each stage of the process and explain what each screen is asking you to do.

"All you have to do is connect your device to a power source and press a button"

Activation Prepare your iPad

01 Unlock your device
When you first switch on your iPad you will be presented with a plain-looking lock screen with a slider at the bottom. Tap and hold the slider and swipe it to the right to unlock the iPad.

02 Select your language
You will be presented with a long list of different languages. The language you choose here will be the language that your device is set to and the language that all text will be presented in.

03 Select your Country or Region
Now select your Country or Region. This will determine the apps that are available in the App Store and the various media available from the iTunes app, as well as the correct currency.

Exploring your Home screen

Once your iPad has been set up, start exploring

Your Settings
Your first port of call should be the Settings app. Tap on this to start modifying and customising certain aspects of your device

Your Dock
The Dock is a row of app icons in a strip at the bottom of the screen. This Dock is present no matter which of your screens you're on and should be used for your most-used apps

Your apps
A selection of Apple apps are built in to the operating system and will appear on your Home screen as standard. Tap on an icon to launch the app

Adding apps
The Dock contains four apps as standard but you can add an extra one by tapping and holding on an icon until it starts to shake and then dragging it with your finger into the Dock

Tweaking options
If you couldn't decide whether to activate certain services such as Find My iPad and iCloud during the initial setup process then you can do it later. Just tap on your Settings app and you will find the relevant options there to activate and start using these features.

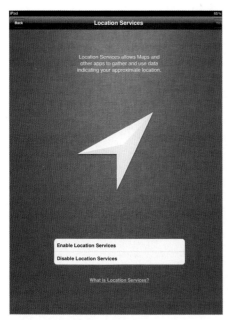

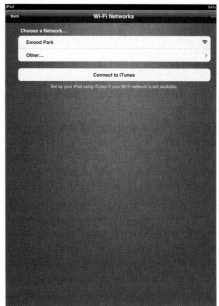

04 Location Services
The next part of the process is dedicated to your device's Location Services. This allows apps to gather and use data indicating your approximate location. This is useful if you lose your device.

05 Enable or disable
You can either enable or disable Location Services. If you are unsure of the purpose of this feature and need more information then don't worry; you can activate it later from Settings.

06 Connect to a network
Your iPad relies on a Wi-Fi network to be able to connect to the internet and fuel a wealth of different services. If you are within range of a Wi-Fi network then it will be detected.

Setting up

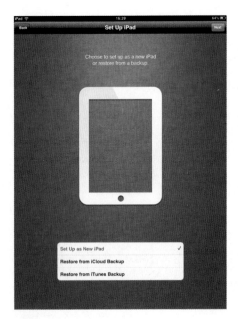

07 Set up iPad

The next screen presents you with three options. You can either set up the device as a new iPad, which is what you'll be doing, or restore it from previous settings backed up to iCloud or iTunes.

08 Sign in

You'll need your own Apple ID to enjoy the main features of your iPad, such as being able to download apps, music and media and back up and sync your data and settings with iCloud.

09 Enter Apple ID

If you have an Apple ID you can tap 'Sign In with an Apple ID' or create one by tapping the 'Create a Free Apple ID' option. If you choose the latter you will be guided through the creation process.

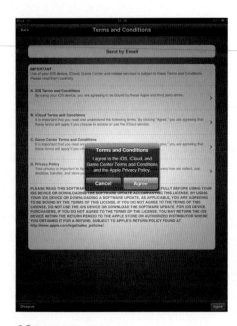

10 Read the T&Cs

After signing in, you will be presented with a screen of Terms and Conditions that relate to all aspects of your iPad and the services that you will be using, such as iCloud, Game Center and so on.

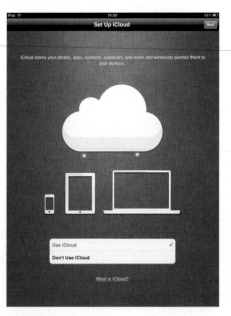

11 Set up iCloud

Apple's iCloud was new to iOS 5 and is even better in iOS 6. It allows you to back up data from your iPad to your own cloud storage space. Opt in to the service here; it won't cost you anything.

12 Find My iPad

If you misplace your iPad then Find My iPad will help you locate it on a map, play a sound or display a message. You can activate this service to sync the location of your device with your iCloud.

Exploring your Settings

Start personalising your iPad through Settings

The categories
All of the categories to which the Settings apply will be presented in a list on the left-hand side of the screen. Tap an option to bring up its individual screen of settings

Side Switch
The switch on the side of your device can be used for muting sound or locking your screen rotation. The latter is very useful and you can assign it from the 'General' Settings section

All about your iPad
By tapping on the 'About' option in the 'General' section, you can get in-depth info on your device, such as the serial number, capacity and the amount of space that your various apps and media take up

Software Update
By tapping on the 'Software Update' option in the 'General' section your device will be able to find and update your iOS, without the need to connect your device to a computer

Restoring from backup
You may not be setting up a brand new iPad; you may just be restoring your existing iPad using an iCloud backup. In which case the setup process is still carried out the same way, but when you're asked to set up your iPad, choose 'Restore from iCloud Backup' and all of your previous settings will be restored and all of your apps and media will be redownloaded – it may take a while though.

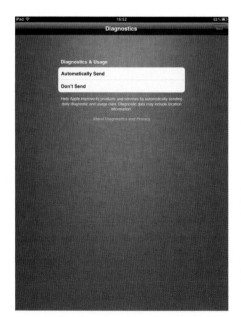

13 Diagnostics & Usage
Apple likes to keep track of how its products are performing, so this screen allows you to send diagnostic data straight to Apple. Opt for 'Don't Send' to keep your information private.

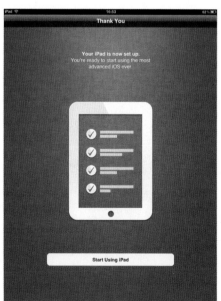

14 Set up complete
Congratulations! You have now worked your way through the entire set-up process. A screen will confirm the process is complete, so what are you waiting for? Tap on the 'Start Using iPad' button!

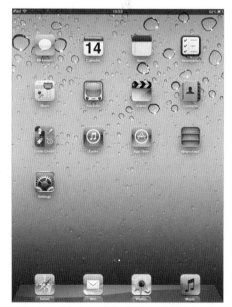

15 Start using your iPad
You'll be presented with your Home screen, so start tapping on icons to launch apps and find your way around, experimenting with the gestures needed to operate your new device.

Setting up

Set up iCloud and start syncing

All of your documents can be moved wirelessly from device to device without you having to lift a finger

 With iOS 5 came iCloud, a new service from Apple that is so much more than just a hard drive in the sky. Free to all iOS 5 and iOS 6 users, iCloud automatically and securely stores your content so that it's always available on your iPad, iPhone, Mac… whatever device you're using. Through iCloud you get full access to your music, apps, photos and documents, and it also wirelessly syncs all of your emails, contacts and calendars to keep them up to date across all of your devices.

When you sign up for iCloud you get 5GB of free storage, which is plenty because all of your music, apps, books, and photos that are pushed to all of your devices don't count against your free storage. And seeing as your mail, documents, account info, settings and other app data don't use up much space, you'll find that your free quota goes a long way. You can now set up iCloud when you register, but if you opted not to or you registered your iPad before the iOS 5 update, follow these steps to set up iCloud now.

"When you sign up for iCloud you automatically get 5GB of free storage"

iCloud   Setting up your personal iCloud

01 Update to iOS 5 or iOS 6
iCloud comes as part of iOS 5, so connect your device to your computer through iTunes and check to ensure that you have either iOS 5 or iOS 6 software installed on your device.

02 Launch Settings
There is very little tinkering to do to set up your iCloud. Start off by launching your Settings app, and in the column on the left-hand side of the screen will be a section called 'iCloud'. Tap on this.

03 Sign in
To activate your iCloud account you will need to log in using your Apple ID, which is the same email address and password that you use for your other services, such as iTunes and the App Store.

Your iCloud Settings

Activating your free iCloud account is simple and easy to manage

Storage & Backup

You can select the option to automatically back up your iPad to iCloud under certain conditions and purchase more storage space if you need it

Delete Account

If you are upgrading your device and wish to disassociate your current iPad with an iCloud account then simply tap the 'Delete Account' option

Your account

Your free iCloud is activated when you enter your Apple ID. This is the same email address and password that you use for other Apple services, like iTunes

Compatible apps

iCloud is integrated into a host of default Apple apps and works behind the scenes to make sure everything is synced across all devices

Documents in the Cloud

One of the best features of iCloud, Documents in the Cloud, enables you to work on Pages, Numbers or Keynote documents on your iPad and then, without the need to save or manually transfer them, your documents will automatically appear on your iPhone or Mac for you to work on later. Enable the 'Documents & Data' option in your iCloud Settings to make it so.

04 Merge data

If you've already set up an iCloud account on another device, then you will be asked if you'd like to merge data, such as calendars, with the data that exists on the iCloud. Choose 'Merge'.

05 Start syncing

Select which of the apps utilise the service, such as Mail, Contacts, Calendar, Reminders, Safari Bookmarks, Notes, Photo Stream and Documents & Data. Move the sliders to activate the apps.

06 Automatic downloads

To get the most out of iCloud, click on the Store section in Settings and then turn on 'Automatic Downloads' for Music, Apps and Books to download all new purchases from other devices.

Get to know the iTunes interface

iTunes has morphed from a program designed to look after your music library to one capable of storing any media you'd care to enjoy, all while being the gateway to Apple's online store

The first version of iTunes was released over a decade ago, back on 9 January 2001. Apple had purchased Casady and Greene's SoundJam MP two years previously, realising that it had missed the boat with regards to the CD ripping and burning that was going on at the time. Back then, the iPod didn't even exist. Three years later, the iTunes Music Store was born, along with Apple's ambitions as an online entertainment retailer.

It's only recently that you can actually use your iPad without first installing iTunes on your computer, and since the release of iOS 5 you can activate your device and get all the latest system updates without the need to manually connect it to your computer. However, there is a lot more to iTunes than allowing iPad functionality, not least the ability to convert your CD collection to MP3 format and copy the tracks to your device, browse for all the latest entertainment and apps at the iTunes and App Stores and enjoy the many new features that iCloud provides. Here we show you the basics.

> "It's only recently that you can actually use your iPad without installing iTunes"

iTunes Getting to know the software

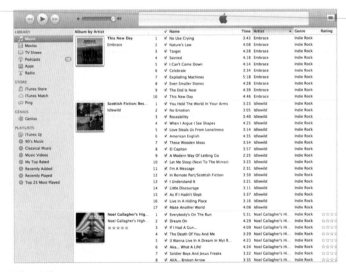

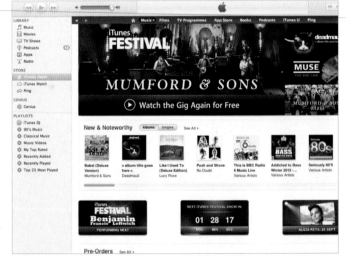

The Library

Your media is broken down by type, like music, films, television shows, podcasts, books and apps for your iOS devices, all of which you can acquire from the iTunes Store. The last one on the list, Radio, lets you listen to online radio stations for free.

The Store

To access Apple's online media store, move your cursor to the Store section in the Sidebar and click on iTunes Store. The front page is geared towards entertainment, showing you the latest and most popular songs and albums, films and TV shows (books can only be purchased from your iOS device).

Browsing the App Store

Helping you find the apps you need in seconds

Categories
Narrow down your search by browsing through a specific category. To access this menu, click on the small triangle to the right of 'App Store'

Search and find
If none of these are of any help, you can always use the good old-fashioned search field. Start typing and a list of options will appear for you to choose from

Latest releases
Sometimes a recommendation is all you need, and the New & Noteworthy section shows you a selection of staff favourites that you may feel suit your exact needs

Top Charts
Looking at the bestselling apps can help you decide what to get. This one on the front page shows the top sellers irrespective of their category (categories also have their own charts)

How do I choose what to add to my iPad?

By default, iTunes is designed to take care of that for you: even if you have more media than can fit in your iPad, it'll choose which ones to add, and which to leave behind. But if you'd like more control over the process, start by clicking on the iPad in the Devices section. From there, you'll have options in the various tabs to select which songs, films or apps you'd like to include. There are multiple ways of doing this, which will be explained in other parts of this book.

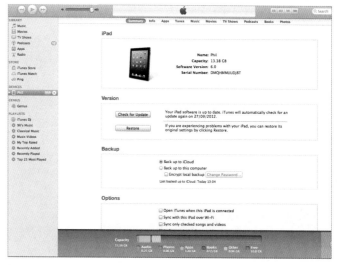

Finding the apps

To get to the App Store and start browsing for programs for your iPad, check out the menu bar, top of the main part of the iTunes interface, and click on App Store. Once there, you'll find two buttons at the top, one labelled iPhone, the other iPad. Click on iPad.

Connecting your iPad

After activating your iPad, it'll appear in the Sidebar under the Devices section. Click on its name and you'll gain access to your device. You can use that section to select which media to add and which apps to install, or just let iTunes add everything automatically.

Sync your music collection

Here's how easy it is to sync your music collection from a computer to the iPad

It might not exactly be pocketable, but the iPad is easily Apple's best music player to date. Its 9.7-inch Retina display makes it easy to browse the music library, album artwork looks gorgeous when viewed full-screen, and the Library found in the desktop version makes a comeback, giving quick access to podcasts, audiobooks, genius mixes and more. We can say with confidence that the iPad is the most fun way to listen to music.

Getting music onto your iPad is a simple process through iTunes. It's possible to sync tracks, albums or your entire music library. iTunes remembers your settings, so whenever your iPad is plugged in to the computer it automatically syncs any new music tracks to the device. By spending just a few minutes setting up your music sync options, you'll never have to manually transfer tracks and albums again.

iTunes Get your music on your iPad

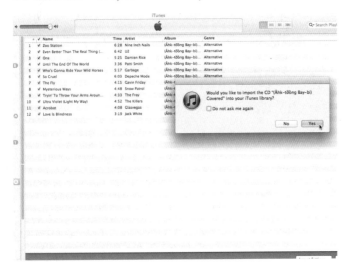

01 Import tunes

First, ensure you have music tracks in your iTunes Library. Insert a CD into the drive and you will be asked if you want to import it. Click 'Yes'.

02 Get to your music

Connect your iPad to your computer and then you can either drag songs manually from your library to your device or click on the 'Music' tab.

03 Choose what to sync

From here you can choose what to sync. Once you're happy with the selection, click the Apply/Sync button at the bottom of the screen.

04 Get playing

Once the syncing process has been completed, turn on your iPad and open the Music app located in the dock at the bottom of the screen.

Sync movies onto your iPad

We explain how easy it is to copy movies from your desktop computer to an iPad

Movies look amazing on the iPad screen. Whether laying in bed or sitting on a train with the iPad in your hands, the display shows off movies with vivid clarity. It gets even better if the movie has been purchased or rented through the iTunes Store, as the iPad will display detailed information about the film and enable users to skip directly to a particular chapter with just one tap of the finger. For those with an Apple TV it's also possible to wirelessly stream any movie to the device from your iPad, enabling you to watch films on a high-definition TV and control the playback using the iPad's touch screen display, but more on that later.

In this tutorial we'll explain how easy it is to sync movies from your desktop computer to the iPad using iTunes. In next to no time you'll be up and running with a selection of great movies on your iPad.

iTunes Sync your movies to your iPad

01 Get ready
Ensure you have movies to sync in iTunes. Films can be purchased from the iTunes Store, or copied to your iTunes Library in MOV or MP4 format.

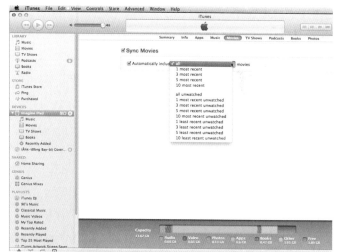

02 Select films
Connect your iPad and click on it in iTunes, then select the Films tab at the top of the screen. If unselected, check the top Sync Films button.

03 Sync!
Select the films that you wish to sync, but keep aware of the file sizes. Once you're happy, click the Apply/Sync button at the bottom of the screen.

04 Get watching
Once the films have copied you can watch them from the Videos app. If purchased from the Store, they will include chapters for easy navigation.

Setting up

Copy TV shows to your iPad

The iPad's perfect for watching programmes on the go. Here's how to sync TV shows from a Mac/PC

With its relatively large 9.7-inch Retina display and lengthy battery life, the iPad is pretty much the perfect portable television. Its screen is large enough to be easily viewed by more than one person and all images look fantastic on its colourful, high-resolution screen. For anyone who travels around a lot, it's the perfect way to keep entertained on long journeys, and because the iPad is so portable you can continue watching wherever you are in your home.

Getting TV shows onto your iPad is a simple process. By opening the iTunes app you can purchase the latest episodes of your favourite show and download them directly to the device. Alternatively it's possible to sync all the shows on your desktop computer to the iPad by using the desktop version of iTunes. Follow us through this tutorial as we explain how easy it is to sync your TV shows in just four steps. You'll have all of your favourite TV programmes ready to watch on your iPad in no time.

iTunes Watch downloaded television shows on your iPad

01 Go shopping
Go to the iTunes Store and then click on the 'TV Programmes' tab at the top. Here you can browse, purchase and download shows to your computer.

02 Plug and sync
Plug your iPad into the computer. Once it has synced, select it from the grey bar on the left. Next, click on TV Programmes at the top of the screen.

03 Select shows
If Sync TV Programmes isn't already checked, tick it to enable syncing. Once you're happy with the selection of TV shows, click the Apply/Sync button.

04 Get watching
You can view TV shows from the Videos app on your iPad. Simply open the app and you'll see a TV Shows button at the top of the screen.

Sync podcasts onto your iPad

Discover how to sync podcasts from your desktop computer to an iPad

Think of podcasts as individual radio shows without the music – some are a few minutes long, others hours in length, and they can be listened to from within the Music app on your iPad. Once you've found a great podcast it's possible to subscribe to it from the iPad's iTunes app, enabling your desktop computer or iPad to automatically download the latest episodes as soon as they're available, ready for you to enjoy. With podcasts you can pick and choose the subjects that interest you, enabling you to skip the annoying adverts and subject matters that you normally sit through when listening to the radio.

In this tutorial we'll explain how to subscribe to podcasts and sync them between your desktop computer and iPad. It's a simple process done entirely through iTunes. Once you've subscribed to a handful of podcasts you'll find yourself with hours of free entertainment, and wondering how you ever lived without them.

iTunes Listen to podcasts on your iPad

01 Download new podcasts
Open iTunes on your Mac or PC, click on the iTunes Store button then choose Podcasts from the menu at the top of the screen.

02 Plug and sync
Once you've got the podcasts, plug your iPad into your Mac/PC. Click your iPad from the grey side panel, then the Podcasts button at the top.

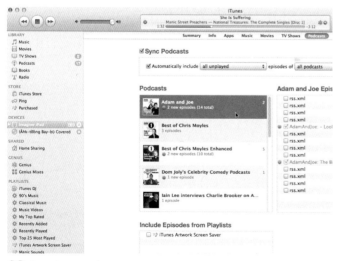

03 Syncing options
From the Podcasts window you can choose to sync individual podcasts, entire subscriptions or only the podcasts with new episodes available.

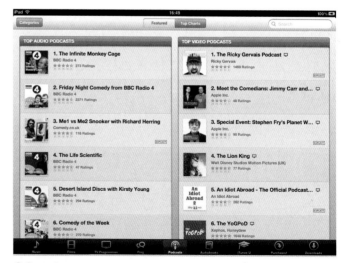

04 Podcasts on your iPad
You can play synced podcasts from the Music app. To get podcasts without a Mac/PC, open the iTunes app and you'll find a Podcasts button.

Sync books with your iPad

Find out how to sync books with your iPad, and where to download the latest titles

Before the iPad was even announced, media pundits were declaring it to be the saviour of print media. Now that it's been in the hands of customers for a year, it's beginning to justify that claim, as the iPad is a fantastic device for reading books and magazines for a number of reasons. Its large 9.7-inch display makes reading text a joy, particularly when combined with the Retina display on the new iPad; the vivid colour screen makes images look even better than their printed counterparts; its support for multimedia means

videos and web links can be embedded in books; and it's possible to change the font and text size, look up words with a dictionary and easily control the brightness for when reading in a low-lit environment. The list goes on.

eBooks can either be synced from a desktop computer or purchased directly from Apple's iBooks app – and if downloading books to your computer, you can also use the 'Automatic Downloads' iCloud feature (go to Settings>Store and activate the options). Here we show you how to sync from iTunes.

iTunes Sync eBooks to your iPad

01 Go shopping
Go to the iTunes Store and click on the 'Books' tab at the top of the screen. Books you purchase and download will be added to 'Books' in your library.

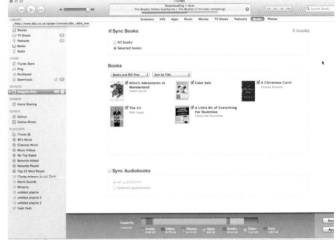

02 Books window
Turn on your iPad and plug it into the computer. After syncing, click on your iPad from the grey side bar, then the Books option at the top of the screen.

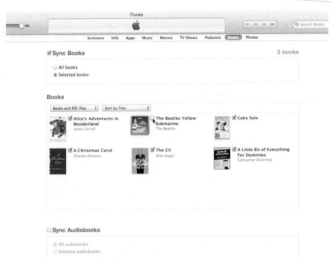

03 Choose your books
You can sync every book by checking the All Books button, or alternatively select your books of choice. Click the Sync/Apply button once you're ready.

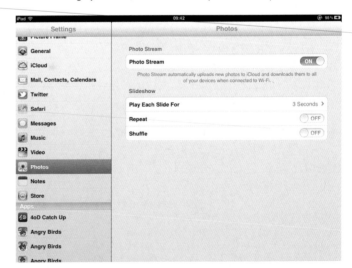

04 Download in iBooks
If you install the free iBooks app on your iPad then you can also download books from within by tapping the 'Store' button in the top-right corner.

Sync photos on your iPad

Discover how easy it is to sync photographs from your Mac/PC to an iPad

The iPad is the perfect device for displaying photos. Thanks to its Multi-Touch support it's easy to swipe through images, zoom into areas and create slide-shows. It's by far the best way to show off your latest holiday snaps as the device can be passed from person to person, and because the Photos app is so intuitive it can be used by anyone – even children.

There are a handful of ways to get your favourite photos onto your iPad. They can be synced from a Mac/PC, emailed or imported from an SD card and, thanks to the wonder of iCloud's Photo Stream feature, even beamed wirelessly to your device automatically. In this tutorial we'll explain how easy it is to transfer batches of images from your computer using iTunes.

iTunes Get your photos on your iPad via iTunes

01 Plug in
Open iTunes on your Mac/PC, then plug the iPad into the computer and they'll sync. Once done, click on your iPad from the grey side bar on the left.

02 iPad summary
You'll see a summary of your iPad. At the top of the screen are various buttons for syncing media – click on the Photos button at the far end.

03 Choose your photos
Here you'll see an option to sync photos from your Mac or PC. Click on the check box and choose a folder from your computer. When correct, click OK.

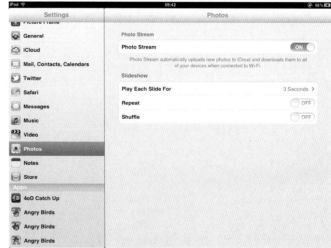

04 Activate Photo Stream
To get all photos automatically pushed to your iPad from your computer or iPhone, go to Settings>Photos and turn Photo Stream on.

Setting up

App used: Settings

Time needed: 5 minutes

Use iPad Settings to suit your needs

The Settings app is the epicentre of your iPad. Here you can customise everything from how apps work to the look and feel of the display

 On the first page of the iPad screen is an app called Settings. This controls how your iPad works, allows individual apps to be configured and sets the look and feel of the screens. With it, you can enforce security, log on to Wi-Fi networks, save battery power, add signatures to emails, configure the web browser Safari to use specific search engines and much, much more. It is, perhaps, the most important app on your iPad. Learn what it has to offer and how you can change or configure things and you will take control of the iPad to make it work the way you want it to.

In this tutorial we are going to introduce you to some of the key features within Settings – the ones that you may want to check out straight away to get yourself acquainted to the system. More specific tutorials will follow to show you functions in more depth, but for now, let's delve into the nerve centre of this incredible piece of kit.

"Learn what the Settings have to offer and make the iPad work the way you want it to"

Settings
Work your way around the iPad's control system

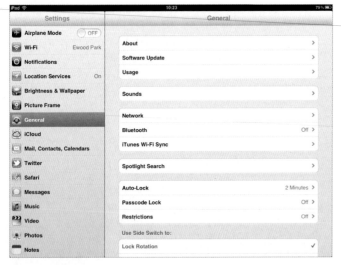

Go to Settings
Turn your iPad on and slide the bar across to unlock it. On the very first screen is the Settings app. Tap once on it to launch. There are a great number of parameters but you'll find a lot of useful things to tweak in the 'General' section. If this isn't automatically selected, tap on it now.

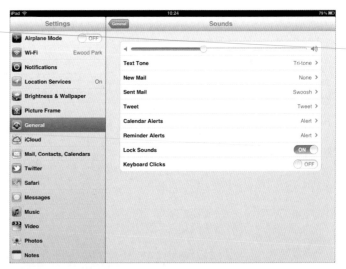

Change the sounds
One of the first things to check out is the sound settings; tap on Sounds and customise these options by sliding the setting to On or Off and sliding your finger along the volume to change it. The General section also lets you control Bluetooth, Date & Time settings and much more so explore here.

The Settings menu laid out in full

Work your way around this user-friendly settings menu

Wireless updates
With iOS 6 you no longer need to connect your iPad to a computer in order to update the system software. Just choose 'Software Update' do get the latest iOS (if available) beamed directly to your device

Master the options
The Settings app controls lots of different features of the iPad and they are all available simply by tapping on the entry for each one and then making the changes required. Some of the most useful include using a graphic equaliser with your music, different fonts with Notes and selecting from Google, Yahoo! Or Bing as your search engine in Safari. To set the music preference, tap on the iPod entry and then on EQ and you can select from a range of music styles and also boost or reduce the base and optimise for speech.

Location, Location
Tap on this section to turn on or off the location services. This allows the iPad to find your co-ordinates using GPS, Wi-Fi and cellular data for things like the Map app

Lock settings
Use Auto-Lock to decide how long you want the iPad to wait for inactivity before it locks, and use Passcode Lock if you want to set a password for when you turn on your iPad

Multitasking Gestures
Here you can turn on or off multitasking gestures, which allow you to use certain swipes of your fingers, such as swipe up, left, right or pinch with four or five fingers, to control your iPad

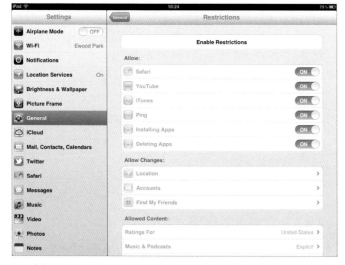

Enable Restrictions
The General section also has one of the most important settings options, especially if you let your kids play with the iPad. Here you can turn off in-app purchases, access to iTunes and much more. Just tap Enable Restrictions and you are prompted to set a passcode. Make it memorable.

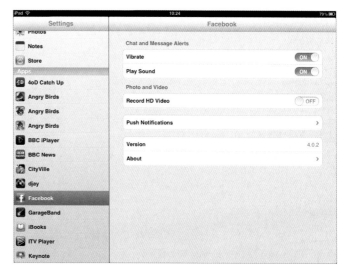

App Settings
The Settings menu also lets you change the options for any apps you have downloaded. Just tap on the app you want to change the settings on and you have access to the options. As usual, move sliders to On or Off depending on your preferences to that function.

App used:
Mail

Time needed:
5 minutes

Access email on your iPad

While email works perfectly well on the iPhone it really comes into its own on the iPad's larger screen. This handy tutorial will let you set up your own personal account

 In today's digital age using email is one of the most essential ways of being able to stay in touch with friends and family, as well as being a pretty vital tool in the business world. While both the iPhone and iPod touch are perfectly capable of displaying email, the iPad is just so much better due to its larger size, making it a much superior option. The virtual keyboard makes it far easier and quicker to type on (especially when you need to write longer mails) making it far more practical to use.

This step-by-step tutorial will not only show you how to set up a new or existing email account for use on the iPad and beyond, but will also take you through the fundamentals of reading and sending email. Once set up you'll be able to use existing accounts at will, quickly reply and forward mail that you receive, and, most importantly, ensure that you stay in touch with friends and loved ones. Basically you will never look at your iPad in the same way again.

"You will never look at your iPad in the same way again"

Mail Set up an email account on your iPad

01 Set things up

In order to set up an email account you will need to first enter the Settings of your iPad. Look at the icons on the first page of your iPad until you find one with a large cog and two smaller cogs. Tap on it to continue to the Settings menu.

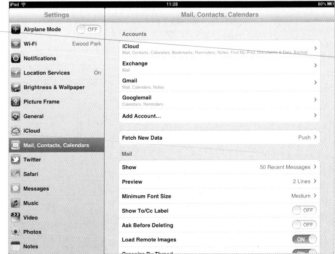

02 Find your mail

Upon entering Settings you'll find a row of different icons down the left-hand side of the screen. Look for and select 'Mail, Contacts, Calendars' in order to continue. Now look on the right-hand side of the screen and tap on Add Account…

Viewing mail

Look for the mail tab on the left-hand side of the page in Mail. Tap on it and you will instantly be shown your latest mail. Scroll down for more emails

Forwarding Mail
If you need to reply to an email hit the arrow icon near the top of the screen. You can then reply to the sender or forward the message on

Move items
Want to organise your mail? Simply tap the folder icon located at the top of the screen. You can then send your mail to a variety of different folders

Send email
Tap the tab in the top right-hand corner of your iPad to send mail. Fill out the address, add a subject and write your mail. Hit send when you're finished

Adding more accounts
If you have the need for additional accounts (perhaps a work account or the account of your significant other) it's relatively easy to add them. All you need to do is re-follow the previous steps for setting up an account. Once you've done that when you enter your mail you will see an 'Accounts' tab in the top left-hand side of the screen. Simply tap on this tab to be taken to all the other accounts set up on your iPad. Select the one you want and you can instantly access your other mail. Very handy.

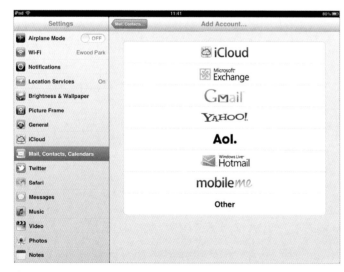

03 Make your choice
You'll now be presented with six different account options. They are Microsoft Exchange, MobileMe, Google Mail, Yahoo! Mail, AOL and Other (which will allow you access to accounts like Hotmail). Whether you want to create a new account or add an existing one, the process is as follows…

04 You've got mail!
After choosing your account you'll be presented with the following screen. All you need to do here is fill in the relevant information for each section. Once this is done simply tap on Save in the top right-hand corner. Congratulations, you have mail.

Setting up

Use iCloud to back up your iPad

With iCloud, you can back up all of your important iPad data to your own virtual hard drive

Your iPad is like a bank vault where all kinds of important stuff is stored. So what happens if your iPad gets lost or goes awry? Nothing, that's what. Thanks to iCloud, all of your data is automatically backed up and kept safely in your own cloud storage space. When your iPad is connected to a power source and a Wi-Fi network, all of your media, photos, videos, settings, app data and messages are backed up.

When you set up a new iOS device or need to restore the information on the one you already have, iCloud Backup does all the heavy lifting. All you have to do is ensure that your device is connected to Wi-Fi, enter your Apple ID and all of your important data will appear on your device without you having to worry about a thing. As you will have read elsewhere in this book, the benefits of using iCloud are vast, and the way in which it goes about its business in the background without you having to worry is just another prime example of how Apple is striving to make your life easier.

"Another prime example of how Apple is striving to make your life easier"

---

iCloud   Activate iCloud and back up your data

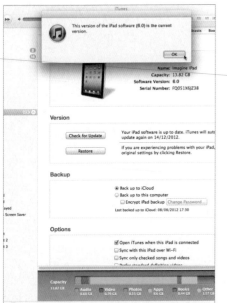

01 Update to iOS 5 or iOS 6

iCloud comes as part of iOS 5 or iOS 6, so connect your device to your computer through iTunes and check to ensure you have the latest free software update installed on your device.

02 Launch Settings

From your iPad's Home screen, launch your Settings app, and in the left-hand column will be a new category called 'iCloud'. Tap on this and then enter your Apple ID and password.

03 Set up

Once your personal iCloud has been set up and you have selected which apps you would like to sync, tap on the 'Storage & Backup' option at the bottom of the list.

Backing up with iCloud

Once activated, your iCloud will back up your stuff automatically

Manage your space
You can see how your free 5GB allocation of cloud storage space is used by tapping on the 'Manage Storage' option

Instant backup
You can back up your data by tapping the 'Backup Now' option. Do this if you change your settings or buy new media

Progress bar
When your device is backing up, a progress bar will appear that shows how far along the process it is. You can cancel the backup at any time

Backup
When the 'iCloud Backup' option is turned on, all settings, documents, media and photos will be automatically backed up when your device is connected to a power supply and Wi-Fi

Manage your storage
By tapping on the 'Storage & Backup' option in the iCloud Settings screen and then going to 'Manage Storage', you'll be able to see exactly how your iCloud is used with individual breakdowns of how much of your free 5GB of space your apps use. If you find that you need to purchase more space then you can do so through this screen.

04 Turn on Backup

On this screen you will be able to monitor and manage your iCloud storage space, but more importantly you will see an option called 'iCloud Backup'. Ensure that the slider is moved to 'On'.

05 Wait for the activation

You'll be presented with a message saying that your iPad will no longer sync to iTunes when connected to your computer, so tap 'OK' and wait for a minute while the Backup feature is activated.

06 Start backing up

Your iPad will now back up when connected to a power source and a Wi-Fi network, but you can perform the backup whenever you want by accessing this screen and tapping 'Backup Now'.

Getting started

All the basics are covered right here to get you in control of your iPad

"Personalise your Notification Center and tailor all aspects of how your device gets messages to you"

48 Move icons and create folders

54 Safari's iCloud tabs

79 Find your way with Maps

92 Explore iTunes

App used:
N/A

Time needed:
3 minutes

Move icons and use folders

Once you've installed lots of apps, the screens start to fill up and it gets harder to find things. Discover how to organise your apps and keep your iPad tidy

Whenever a new app is installed, it just gets added to the end of the existing list, or if there's a gap anywhere, it can appear there. This is fine when you only have a handful of apps, but after a couple of months with your iPad, the screens start to fill up and it all looks disorganised and messy. Fortunately it can all be organised into areas of similar functions, such as games on one page, utilities on another and reference apps on a page as well. You can reorganise your iPad screens using iTunes, where it is easy to create extra screens, even if the current ones are full, but it's also possible to move icons around directly on the iPad. Also, you can create as many folders as you like and bundle apps together to make your display very neat and tidy. The final benefits are that unwanted apps can be deleted and must-have apps can be added to the favourites bar at the bottom of every screen.

"You can bundle apps together to make your display very neat and tidy"

Home screen Keep your iPad organised

01 Activate the wiggle

Turn your iPad on so that you are looking at your Home screen. If you have lots of apps then the icons for them will be spread over subsequent screens. To arrange them together tap and hold an app you want to move until all the apps start to wiggle.

02 Move the app

Still holding down on the app, drag your finger to the edge of the screen you want to move to. The apps will then scroll sideways to give you the next screen. Move your finger over the place you want the app to go and then let go of it.

Inside the new folder display

Edit the folder name and move apps inside it

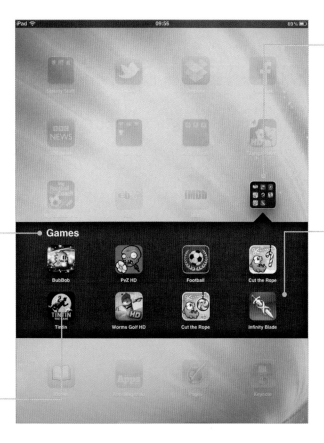

Edit the folder name
Tap a folder to open it. Tap and hold an app inside to go into wiggle editing mode. You can now remove or change the folder name

Take an app out
While in wiggle mode you can drag an app out of the folder again simply by tapping and holding and then moving outside the folder area

Rearrange apps inside the folder
If there's lots of apps inside a folder, rearrange them by tapping and holding and then dragging to a new position. The other apps will shuffle along and move

Delete an app in a folder
To remove an app that is inside a folder simply tap on the 'X' icon on the top-left corner. You will still have a backup inside iTunes

Favourite and unwanted apps
When in wiggle mode a little cross appears on the top-left corner of all the apps. Tap on this to delete the app directly from your iPad. You can't delete the ones the iPad comes with. The favourites bar at the bottom of the screen comes with six slots for your favourite apps. Again, in wiggle mode you can move them around, drag them on or off the bar or simply add your new, favourite app to the ones there by dragging and releasing the app over it

03 Create folders for common apps
Press the Home button to return your iPad to normal. To create folders though, drop an app over the top of one you want it to appear in a folder with. A folder is then instantly created with a name that reflects the type of apps if they are fairly similar.

04 Rename the folder
If the folder name isn't to your liking, simply tap on the 'X' icon to delete it and tap in the text field to enter your own. When complete, press the Home button twice to exit. To add more apps to the same folder, simply drag and drop them into it.

App used: Safari   Time needed: 15 minutes

New Safari features in iOS 6

Apple hasn't forgotten to give its default web browser a quick feature upgrade; here we reveal the most useful upgrades you'll wonder how you did without

Safari has long been considered one of the best mobile browsers. It mixes a simple user interface with great functionality and plenty of additional features to keep everybody happy. Apple isn't a company to stand still, and the iOS 6 rollout predictably saw Safari gain a few new handy features.

The main update involves the continued move to cloud computing and the aim of seamlessly syncing between various devices. To do so, Apple has introduced iCloud Tabs. With the new update, you'll never need to email a link to yourself. Flicking through a webpage on your iPhone at work, but you want to view it on your iPad's 9.7-inch screen at home? iCloud Tabs ensures that a webpage is instantly loaded in any browser linked with your iCloud account.

iCloud Tabs is just the tip of the iceberg though. There's a new Offline Reading List function that lets you view webpages regardless of your internet connection, while much-requested Facebook integration has also been added. Here we take you through those updates in a bit more detail and a few more to boot.

> "The iOS 6 rollout predictably saw Safari gain a few new handy features"

Safari Explore Safari's new features

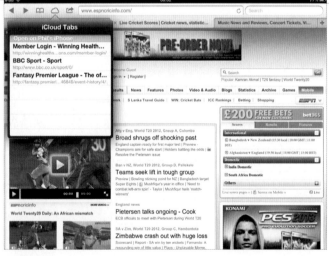

iCloud Tabs

Ensure that all your devices are running with the same iCloud account by using the Settings app on any device. Safari will also need to be activated under the services that are set to sync through your account. iCloud Tabs will appear through the new cloud symbol in your iPad's browser.

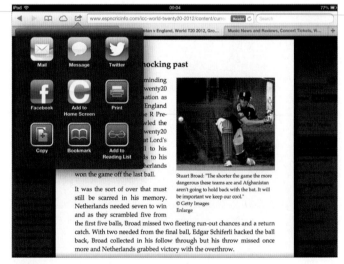

Offline Reading List

In iOS 5, the Reading List was nothing more than a bookmarking system. Now when you save an article for later reading, it's saved to your device so you can view it even if you're offline. Find an article, hit the share icon and tap the Add to Reading List option to get started.

Inside the new Safari
A closer look at the new features

iCloud Tabs
You should be familiar with the silver-lined cloud icon that is now visible on all your devices. It's now a permanent part of Safari on your iPad. Hit this symbol to access the tabs you have open across your devices

Facebook
The world's most famous social network now has its own presence in iOS. Here you have the ability to share articles or webpages to your News Feed. You can add location data and choose who gets to view it

Extra tabs
This may not be something that you will pick up on straight away, but iOS 6 enables you to have more tabs open than ever before. In fact, on your iPad, you'll be able to have 24 tabs open simultaneously

Reading List
On the surface, your Reading List service looks exactly as it did previously. As we've explained, there's a lot more to it now. Hit this tab and you'll be able to view anything you save regardless of your internet connection speed

Keep up to date
Some of iOS 6's main features won't always work without preparation. To use iCloud Tabs you'll need to ensure iCloud is in operation on all devices. Your iPhone and iPod touch will both need to be running iOS 6 for the feature to work. Don't expect everything to work at once. Facebook through Safari won't work unless your iPad has a Facebook account linked to it.

Media uploads
As part of iOS 6, you can upload different types of media without having to leave Safari. In a website that enables you to upload media, like eBay, you'll be automatically taken to your iPad's Camera Roll where you can choose an existing file or opt to create a new picture/video.

Facebook integration
Long overdue, especially considering Twitter's integration as part of the iOS 5 upgrade, Facebook has finally found a built-in place in Apple's mobile operating system. You can share webpages in a matter of seconds; simply hit the Share button and then the iconic Facebook logo to post with a message.

App used: Safari

Time needed: 5 minutes

De-clutter the web with Safari Reader

Thanks to a new Safari feature, you can read fresh web content devoid of intrusive ads and page furniture

 Browsing web pages through Safari on your iPad is a pleasurable experience thanks to its intuitive interface and useful features designed to make surfing the internet as effortless as possible.

The app got even better too, thanks to the iOS 5 update that introduced additional elements such as tabbed pages and Reading List, and has continued to grow in iOS 6. But perhaps one of the best new additions to Safari's arsenal of cool features is Reader.

This feature enables you to read and enjoy web articles free from clutter such as intrusive ad banners and links. If you have accessed a page that can benefit from the Safari Reader function then a 'Reader' icon will be visible in the address bar. Tap on it and the page will undergo an instant transformation into a cleaner, easier-to-read format. What's more, you can increase the font size to make it even easier to read and not get distracted by page furniture. It's quick and easy to use Reader, and when you have read the article and want to return the page to its original state you simply tap the 'Reader' icon again.

"This feature enables you to read and enjoy web articles free from clutter"

Safari How to use Reader

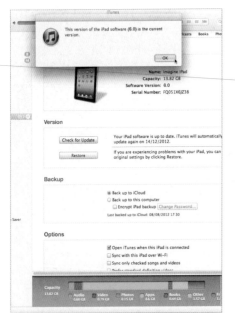

01 Update to iOS 5 or iOS 6

Safari Reader is a service that came as part of iOS 5, so connect your device to your computer through iTunes and ensure that you have either iOS 5 or iOS 6 software installed.

02 Launch Safari

Launch your Safari app and then start browsing. As you access various pages, keep an eye on the address bar for the tell-tale 'Reader' icon that signifies that the page you are on is compatible.

03 Tap 'Reader'

When you find a page that displays the 'Reader' icon, tap on the icon to transform the page into a clear, easy-to-read format. All of the side columns, ads and unnecessary clutter will be removed.

Make pages easier to read

Make web articles cleaner with the tap of a button

Reading List
To store the article safely, without having to create a new bookmark, tap on the sharing icon and choose 'Add to Reading List'

Reader icon
When a page is compatible with Reader, look out for the 'Reader' icon in the address bar and tap it to strip the clutter out of the page

Change font
By tapping on the font icon you can increase the size of the display font to make the current article even easier to read

A cleaner look
Pages that are being viewed through Reader feature only the main text, with all side panels and ads stripped out for a fresher, uncluttered look

iCloud compatibility
The latest version of Safari that comes with the iOS 6 update is fully compatible with your iCloud, so all of your bookmarks and Reading List articles will be automatically synced, meaning you can continue exactly where you left off on a different iOS 6 device later.

04 Increase font size
To make the page even easier to read, tap on the font icon in the top-left corner of the page. This will enable you to switch between two font sizes, increasing the size of the display font.

05 Add to Reading List
If you don't have time to read all of the current article, then you can add it to your 'Reading List' to read later. Tap on the sharing icon on the top bar and choose 'Add to Reading List'.

06 Return to normal
When you've read the article, tap on the 'Reader' icon again, which will now be displayed in purple, and your page will return to its previous state and you'll be able to continue browsing as normal.

App used:
Safari

Time needed:
5 minutes

Use Safari's iCloud Tabs

Access your tabs from every device thanks to the power of iCloud and make sure you're always up to date

iCloud has been helping us keep our digital lives in sync since its launch last year, with features like Contact and Calendar sharing helping us stay organised. However, now Safari is getting some updates to help us stay up to date no matter what device we're using.

The built-in browser hasn't seen many updates since iOS 5, but the addition of iCloud Tabs makes it much more functional. The idea is that, once set up, your device will keep track of what is open in tabs on all of your machines. Whether you are browsing a blog on your Mac or reading the latest news on your iPhone, you can see what tabs you have open with the touch of a button, and quickly open them to carry on where you left off. It's a simple concept, but one that's implemented impressively. Safari has also seen the addition of offline reading lists, which enable you to save pages and articles to read later, even without an internet connection. Read on to find out just how useful these features can be for you.

> "You can see what tabs you have open with the touch of a button"

Safari Start using iCloud Tabs

01 Switch it on

To begin you'll first need to ensure you have iCloud activated on your iPad and that the Safari switch is at the On position. You'll then need to make sure you're using the same iCloud account as on your other devices, for the system to work properly.

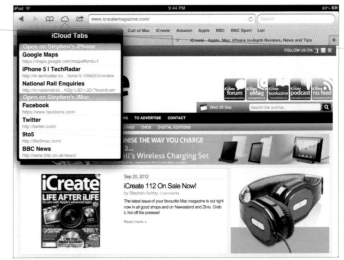

02 View your tabs

Now open up Safari. In the Menu bar you'll see a small iCloud icon next to the Sharing button. Tap it and a drop-down box will appear, showing you all the tabs you have open on the various devices you are using, separated by the device name.

Safari's new features

The best new addition to Safari

Constant updates
These tabs are constantly updated through iCloud. If you're using two devices at once, you will see the tab titles change on the iPad as you click to different pages on the Mac

Offline, wherever
You can save multiple pages to your Reading List and they will be saved across devices. So, saving a site on your Mac for reading later will also save it to your iPad. Once it's been saved, you can read it anywhere you like

iCloud bookmarks
You can also share your Bookmarks between devices. So if you have a series of sites you view on all your devices, you can sync your Bookmarks and then access them with a single tap

Picking up
If you're reading a news story, or just want to show a page you've found to a friend when you're visiting their house, iCloud Tabs is perfect. Find the tab you had open on your Mac and tap it to open

Limited syncing
iCloud Tabs will sync over the tabs you currently have open on your other devices, but they won't sync the internet history for those tabs. If you've ended up on a page on your Mac after several clicks and referrals from different websites, you can't go back through these pages on your iPad. Only the currently open page is visible on other devices, while the history of the whole process is saved on the original device.

03 Reading Lists

Next to the iCloud icon is the Bookmarks icon. Tap it and use the buttons along the bottom of the drop-down menu to navigate to the Reading List. These are all the pages you've saved to read later. They can be viewed offline, which is perfect for long journeys.

04 Sharing and saving

Using the new options from the Sharing menu you can now share an interesting site quickly through Facebook and Twitter, or add it to your Reading List to view later offline. You can even send it to a friend in a message. Sharing in iOS 6 is easier than ever before.

App used: Mail   **Time needed:** 5 minutes

Mail's new features

iOS 6 has brought new features to Apple's Mail app, so managing your emails is even easier

When it comes to the way people use their iPads, one of the main things people do with the tablets is send and read emails. The large touch screen makes it a beautifully simple way to view your mail, and with messages displaying photos inside the message itself, it's much more engaging.

In iOS 6, Apple hasn't changed the formula of Mail too much – the popular app still displays your messages in much the same way, but there have been a few subtle but useful changes that will make emailing much easier.

First, you can now pull your messages down to refresh the list, rather than tapping a button at the bottom of the screen like before. It's a tiny change, but it's so natural that you'll get used to it immediately. It's also now super quick to add images to messages from within the app, saving you the effort of having to send them through the Photos app as you were forced to do before. Finally you have VIPs – this great feature lets you make your friends a VIP. Their messages will appear starred, and will be sorted into a separate inbox with customisable alerts so you know when they've got in touch.

> "The app still displays your messages in much the same way, but there have been a few subtle but useful changes"

Mail Use the new features of Mail

Pull to refresh
If you swipe in from the left-hand side of the screen, you can now pull the list of current emails down – this gesture prompts Mail to check the server for new messages.

VIPs
To make a contact into a VIP, click their name and then choose Add to VIP from the bottom of the list in the drop-down menu. This means you'll be alerted when an email from them arrives.

Multiple signatures
You can also add multiple signatures to your accounts in the Settings app, by choosing Signature and then Per Account, before typing out a signature.

Mail's amazing new features

How will the brand-new features affect you?

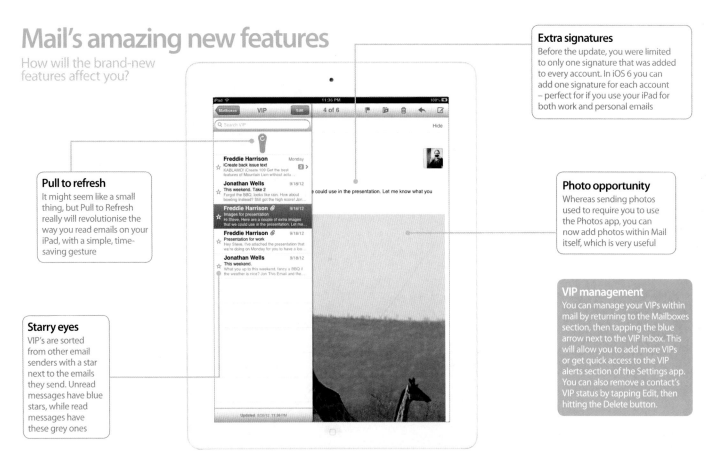

Extra signatures
Before the update, you were limited to only one signature that was added to every account. In iOS 6 you can add one signature for each account – perfect for if you use your iPad for both work and personal emails

Pull to refresh
It might seem like a small thing, but Pull to Refresh really will revolutionise the way you read emails on your iPad, with a simple, time-saving gesture

Photo opportunity
Whereas sending photos used to require you to use the Photos app, you can now add photos within Mail itself, which is very useful

Starry eyes
VIP's are sorted from other email senders with a star next to the emails they send. Unread messages have blue stars, while read messages have these grey ones

VIP management
You can manage your VIPs within mail by returning to the Mailboxes section, then tapping the blue arrow next to the VIP Inbox. This will allow you to add more VIPs or get quick access to the VIP alerts section of the Settings app. You can also remove a contact's VIP status by tapping Edit, then hitting the Delete button.

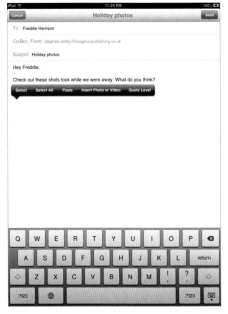

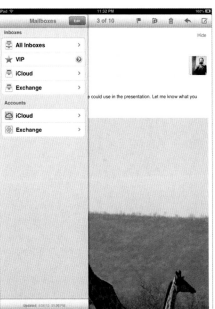

Inline images
It's very easy to add an image to an email; simply double-tap and choose Insert Photo or Video. Then select your image from that pop-up menu and hit Add.

VIP inbox
Swipe in from the left or tap Inbox and you will see a shiny new VIP option. Tap it and you'll be able to view messages from the VIPs you have added to your list.

Customised notifications
You can customise Notifications for VIP messages in the Notifications section of the Settings app. This way you will always know when your VIPs send you an email.

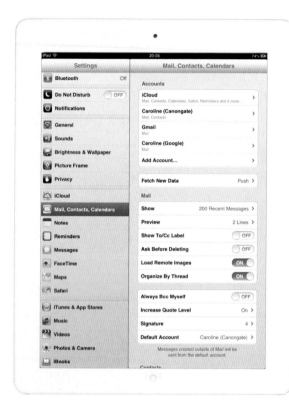

 App used: Mail   **Time needed:** 5 minutes

Set up separate Mail signatures

Organising signatures for each of your email accounts is very easy. Here's how to do it

The person who thought up the concept of email signatures deserves a medal. After all, because they can be automatically added to the end of every email message you send, they cumulatively save countless hours of time that would otherwise be spent typing your name or contact details. Frankly, emails would be a chore without them.

But having a single email signature to choose from is rarely enough. You could, for example have both personal and business email accounts coexisting on your iPad. The formal nature of a business signature would look slightly odd stuck at the bottom of a quick email to your best mate. Equally, if you share your iPad with others in your family you'll each want your own personal signature on the emails that you send.

The ability in iOS 6 to set up separate email signatures on different email accounts is a big plus. It's very easy to do, and you can be up and running in a couple of minutes.

"Having a single email signature to choose from is rarely enough"

Mail Setting up multiple signatures

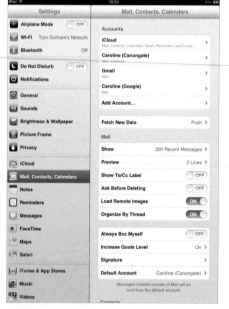

01 Open Settings

Go to Settings and then scroll down the list, tap Mail, Contacts, Calendars. Once you've called up these options for Mail, on the right-hand side, tap the Signature option.

02 Choose your option

Here you have a choice: All Accounts sets a single signature to be used for all accounts and then Per Account allows you to set one for each of your email accounts.

03 Add the signature

Tap Per Account – this will show a box with accounts showing below it. Tap inside the box to enter your personal signature for that specific email account.

Sorting out signatures

Putting your personal
mail signatures in order

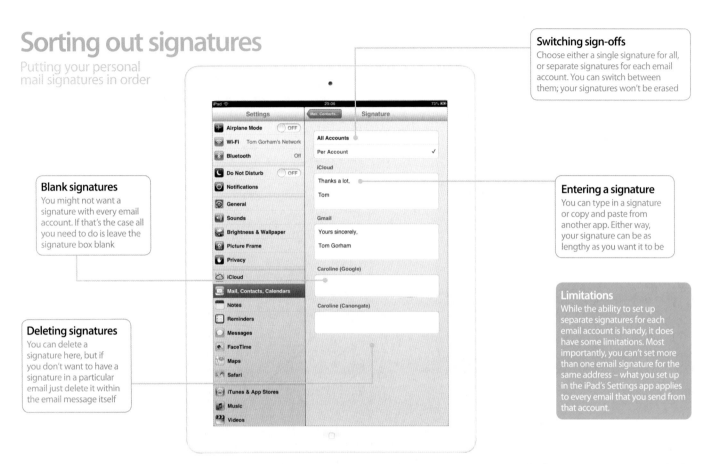

Switching sign-offs
Choose either a single signature for all,
or separate signatures for each email
account. You can switch between
them; your signatures won't be erased

Blank signatures
You might not want a
signature with every email
account. If that's the case all
you need to do is leave the
signature box blank

Entering a signature
You can type in a signature
or copy and paste from
another app. Either way,
your signature can be as
lengthy as you want it to be

Deleting signatures
You can delete a
signature here, but if
you don't want to have a
signature in a particular
email just delete it within
the email message itself

Limitations
While the ability to set up
separate signatures for each
email account is handy, it does
have some limitations. Most
importantly, you can't set more
than one email signature for the
same address – what you set up
in the iPad's Settings app applies
to every email that you send from
that account.

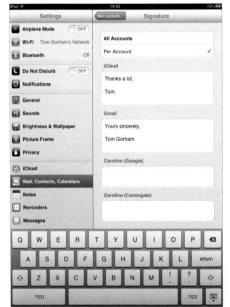

04 Add more signatures

Continue to enter your signature details into the
other boxes for different accounts. If you don't
want to add a signature to a particular account,
just leave it blank.

05 Rich-text signatures

You're not limited to plain text; you can style your
signature with bold or italics by selecting the
word and choosing those options from the popover menu.

06 Using your signatures

When you return to create a message in Mail it
will automatically add you signature, depending
on the specific account that you're sending your
email from.

Getting started

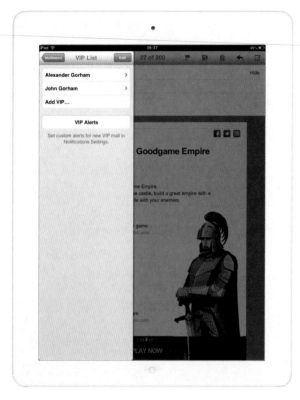

App used:
Mail

Time needed:
5 minutes

Select VIPs in Mail

How do you make sure you don't miss important emails? Set up your important contacts as VIPs, that's how…

For many people, managing their email inbox ends up as a battle that must be fought anew each day. Sifting through the usual cascade of email newsletters and chatter to find the must-see messages from friends or colleagues can be a chore. And as a result, it's all too easy to miss an important email in the process. While it would be great if you could hire a personal assistant to manage your inbox, Mail's new VIP feature is almost as good, and certainly much more affordable.

This feature allows you to choose certain people as very important people, or VIPs. When you have set up your list of VIPs, emails from these contacts will automatically appear in their own section in Mail, which makes it much easier to find the emails that are most important to you.

However, there's more to VIP than simple organisation. When the feature is activated, you'll know straight away when a contact gets in touch. By setting up notification preferences, such as an on-screen alert, or a unique sound, you'll be notified as soon as their email arrives.

"It would be great if you could hire a personal assistant, but Mail's VIP feature is much more affordable"

Mail Manage your VIPs in Mail

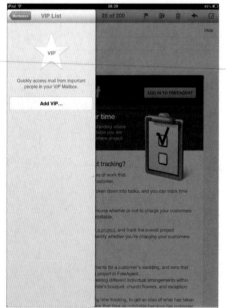

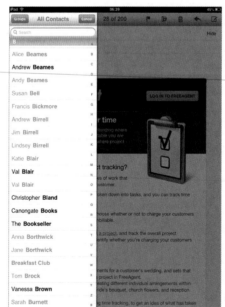

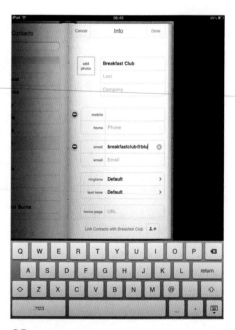

01 Turn a contact into a VIP
Open up Mail, and then in the Mailboxes section you'll see the VIP option. Tap it, and then your VIP list will be revealed. Tap the Add VIP… button to open your list of contacts.

02 Add to the list
Once your list of email contacts is open, all you need to do is tap the name of the contact you'd like to make a VIP – this automatically adds them to your VIP list.

03 Missing VIPs
If the contact isn't visible, or their name is greyed out, this means that you'll have to add an email address for them in the iPad's Contacts app first, before you can make them a VIP in Mail.

Setting up VIP notifications
Choosing alert settings
for important contacts

Choose notification options
The alert options that you choose here will apply only to the contacts in your VIP list. Any other mail alert settings are unaffected

Pick your Alerts
Choose between banner notifications, which go away automatically, and alerts, which require you to dismiss them. Or choose None if you don't want to be notified of a VIP email delivery

Show Preview
Select this option to show a preview of the email on your Home screen when it arrives. You can also preview in the Lock Screen too

Play a sound
If you don't have your eyes on your screen, you can miss an important message. Set a sound to play each time an email from a VIP arrives

Movable settings
VIP settings are stored in the cloud, so those that you set up on the iPad will be recognised on all your iOS 6 devices. If you have a Mac running the latest version of OS X, VIPs appear there too. Mail's VIP section gathers emails from your favourite contacts across multiple email accounts.

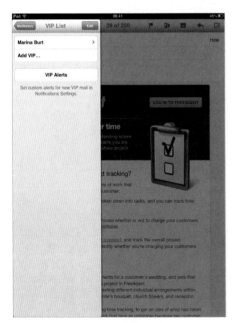

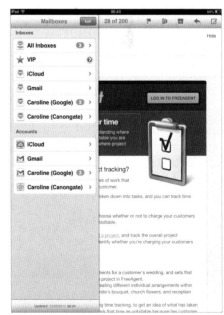

04 Turn on notifications
Head back to the Mail app. When you have finished adding VIPs, you can easily set up a distinctive alert for them. Tap the VIP Alerts button to take you to VIP settings.

05 Set alert options
Make sure the Notification Center slider is set to the On position. You can then choose from the various alerts and special sounds for iPad to play to notify you when a VIP email arrives.

06 Add more VIPs
You can very easily return to add more VIPs in Mail at any time – simply tap the blue arrow button in the Mailboxes section to reopen the VIP list and then repeat the adding process.

App used:
Mail

Time needed:
2 minutes

Add photos and videos to Mail messages

Adding media attachments to emails is no longer a battle;
now it's the work of a couple of clicks

It may be hard to believe but it was once quite a hassle to email images and videos to friends from your iPad. In those dark days, you had to adopt an awkward workaround: open the Photos app, select the video or picture you wanted to send and then email it from within that app. When you think about it, it was an odd way to go about things; surely you should send email attachments from Mail?

Well, in iOS 6, things are more like they should be. You can treat media attachments in the same way as you would in an email application on your computer – by adding them within the body of an email message. With a couple of taps inside your email message, you can open a media browser, add the video or image inside the body of the email, and send it. And while there was once a limitation to the number of videos or images you could send at one time, with Mail in iOS 6 you can add as many as you want.

> "Treat media attachments in the same way as you would in an email app on your computer"

Mail Adding photos or video to email

01 Edit the message

To add a photo or video inside the body of an email, open up the Mail app and tap the Compose button to start a new message. Tap inside the empty body of the message to bring up a popover menu. From this menu, choose 'Insert Photo or Video'.

02 Select the media

You can then choose the video or photo you want to add, either from your Camera Roll or from your Photo Stream. Tap the thumbnail preview of the one you want to add and it will appear in a Preview window. To add it to the email, tap 'Use'.

Adding media to emails
Grabbing images to send by email

Preview images
You preview images in this window before you commit to adding them to the email message. If you like what you see, tap the 'Use' button. If you tap 'Cancel' you can return to choose another image

Inline images
Images or videos that you add appear in the body of the email. You can add more than one image or video to each email

Adding an image
You can tap in an empty area of the body of the email to bring up the popover menu. This lets you add images or videos directly into the body of your email

Adding more
Add more images by double-tapping on an existing image or video. This brings up the popover menu that will let you insert a photo or video nest to the media you just tapped

Using Photos app
Though this new method is great, you can still use the old method of sending media via the Photos app. To do this, open Photos, tap the Edit button, tap the thumbnails of the media you want to send, select the Share button at the bottom and tap the Mail option. That's still handy to know, because the older method has a significant advantage in one area: it's easier to select and add several images quickly. By contrast when you create your message in Mail, you can't add more than one image or media file at a time.

03 Add more images
The image or video should now appear inside your email message. To add more images or videos to the email, just repeat the process in steps 1 and 2, tapping inside the email message and selecting the 'Insert Photo or Video' menu option.

04 Cut images
If you change your mind, you can delete media from your email message. Tap and hold on the image to delete so it's highlighted and then select 'Cut' from the popover menu. When you've finalised your image selection, tap the 'Send' button to send your email.

App used: Calendar   **Time needed:** 10 minutes

Add an event in Calendar

If you find yourself struggling to remember what your schedule for the day, week, month or year looks like, make sure you never miss an important event with your iPad

Tuesday 9 The Calendar app on the iPhone is pretty useful and very easy to use, but it gets dwarfed by the sheer scale of the iPad equivalent. Like the Contacts app, Apple has gone with the classic analogue look and made the app look like an old-school, physical calendar. Of course, this digital version has a multitude of advantages over a real one. Firstly, you get the beauty of typeface rather than scrawled handwriting. Secondly, it's easy to undo mistakes. Thirdly, you can view it in a number of different ways.

Like all the iPad apps, the Calendar app is easy to use. So easy to use that you'll want to document every move you make using it, from eating breakfast to scheduling business meetings. Adding an event is simplicity itself, and the large screen size means that pop-up windows replace the screen shunting right or left as it does on the iPhone. All you need remains in front of you at all times. Once your events are created they can be edited and you can view them in a number of ways as you change orientation or as you dictate on the top tabs of the app.

"You get the beauty of typeface rather than scrawled handwriting"

Adding an event

You're never more than a few taps away from adding or editing an event to your calendar, and the interface is extremely simple

Top tabs
These tabs change the view of the calendar. They are great if you want specific details for a day or an overview of an entire month. Tapping to change them is as intuitive as computing gets

Search
This is a really useful function that negates the need for flipping through countless pages. You just type in a parameter and the app will find what you are looking for

Pop-ups
The size of the screen means that pop-ups can jump from any event whenever you tap them. A great way to view information

Slide navigation
You can navigate through dates on the bottom of the app by sliding your finger or just tapping on a date

Syncing
If you have an iCloud account you can opt to sync calendars when you set up your Mail account. When the iPad is connected to Wi-Fi or 3G it will use the push system to update any other computers or devices linked to your account.

Calendar Add an event

01 Open the app
Open the Calendar app and turn the iPad horizontal to see the dual-page layout. Navigate to the day you want and then tap the plus button on the bottom right.

02 Name your event
A small pop-up window appears in the centre of the screen, as does the keyboard. Tap the field you wish to edit – such as Title – and then name your event.

03 Add details
You can add as much or as little detail as you want, including the location of the event. You have access to a full keyboard so you can go to town on the detail.

04 Give it a date
You now need to add the start and end date of your event, just to make sure you don't miss it! Tap on the relevant field to see the pop-up change into a new window display.

05 Select times
Use the wheels to select the times and dates that you want to use. You can also toggle the 'All-day' button instead if the event that is taking place will take up the entire day.

06 Tap Done
When you have everything in place, you need to tap the Done button located in the top-right corner of the window. Alternatively you can cancel it to return without saving.

07 Set reminders
Tap the Alert field to set reminders for the event. These will help ensure you don't miss an appointment. Alerts pop up on your iPad at the times you set them.

08 Tap it, save it
There are a number of options, ranging from at the event time to two hours before. Tap on the option you wish to use and a tick will appear. Save your progress by clicking Done.

09 Save and view
Save your event and then it will appear on the page. Tap on it to see the full details and to make changes. If you change your mind, tap the red 'Delete Event' button at the bottom.

App used:
Reminders

Time needed:
10 minutes

Never miss an event with Reminders

Thanks to Apple's task management app, you have no excuse for forgetting birthdays

We all like to think that our minds operate like super-computers. As such, we utter the words, "Don't worry, I'll remember…" on an all-too regular basis, only to forget whatever it was we said we'd never forget. To help, Apple has created its own task management app, and it's a cracker.

Reminders lets you organise your life into To Do lists, complete with due dates, notes and reminders to ensure that you never forget when something important is pressing. Simply jot down tasks, record when you need to do them by, then tick each one off as you complete it. Reminders is location-based, so if you need to pick up some groceries from the supermarket, you can be alerted as soon as you pull in to the car park. The app also works with Calendar, Outlook and iCloud, so any changes you make to your Reminders list will update automatically on all of your calendars. In this tutorial, we guide you through the process of setting your own reminders and managing your To Do lists.

"The Reminders app also works with Calendar, Outlook and iCloud"

Reminders Setting yourself reminders

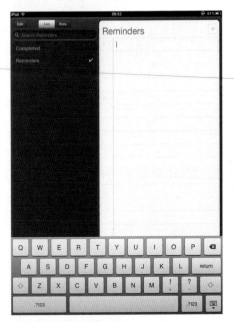

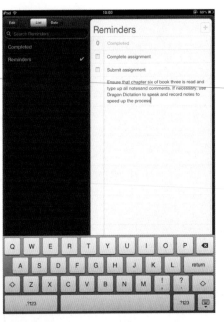

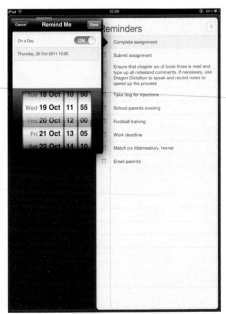

01 Add a reminder
You can immediately start compiling a To Do list by tapping either the paper, or the '+' button in the top-right corner. Use the default keyboard to type your reminder.

02 Make lists
Add reminders to your To Do list by tapping the page or the icon. The lines on the paper will even expand to neatly contain all of your text – just in case you have a complicated task to complete!

03 Add details
Tap a task to view your reminders. Tap Remind Me, slide 'On a Day' to On, then use the trusty wheels and hit the date to choose when your device should alert you.

Adding reminders

Never miss anything you had planned again!

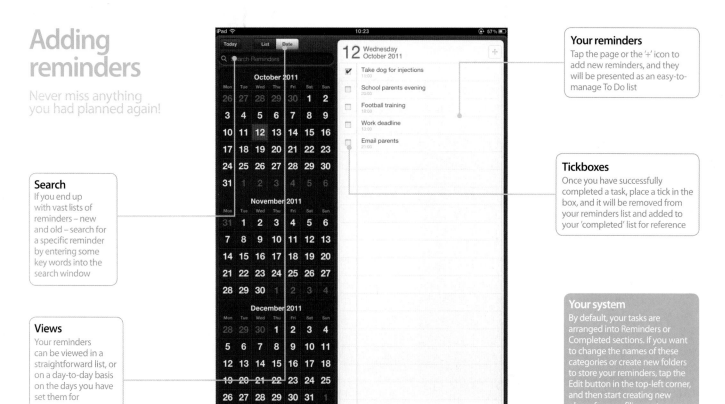

Your reminders
Tap the page or the '+' icon to add new reminders, and they will be presented as an easy-to-manage To Do list

Search
If you end up with vast lists of reminders – new and old – search for a specific reminder by entering some key words into the search window

Views
Your reminders can be viewed in a straightforward list, or on a day-to-day basis on the days you have set them for

Tickboxes
Once you have successfully completed a task, place a tick in the box, and it will be removed from your reminders list and added to your 'completed' list for reference

Your system
By default, your tasks are arranged into Reminders or Completed sections. If you want to change the names of these categories or create new folders to store your reminders, tap the Edit button in the top-left corner, and then start creating new places for your filing system.

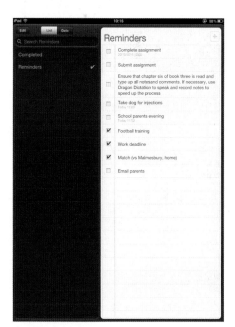

04 More options
You can set various other options, such as the priority, and add notes that relate to each task if you feel you may need more information. Tap Done when you're happy.

05 View as list or date
Your reminders can be categorised by the date. To assign reminders to a specific time period, tap Date, choose which one you wish to assign it to, then add it.

06 Tick them off
Whenever a task is completed, tap the box next to it to add a tick. Reminders that have been ticked will be added to your Completed list, making you feel good about yourself!

Getting started

App used:
Notification Center

Time needed:
10 minutes

Customise your Notification Center

Make sure you never miss a thing by setting up your very own personalised Notification Center

Your iPad has always been good at notifying you about updates, messages, events and so on. However, iOS 6 truly embraces the concept of notifications, and the system introduced in iOS 5 features an enhanced suite to allow you to tailor all aspects of how your device gets messages to you.

Now, you are able to get messages, notifications, news and the latest scores delivered to the top of your screen without disturbing what you are currently doing. All you have to do in order to set up your own personalised Notification Center is go to Settings, choose the apps, and then select the order that they will appear in your Notification Center, and the manner in which they alert you. To stay in the loop, simply swipe down from the top of the screen, and you will be presented with a list of notifications for all of the apps that you have featured. Here, we will show you just how to get the most out of this fantastic feature.

"Tailor all aspects of how your device gets messages to you"

Notification Center How to set up and use your Notification Center

01 Go to Settings
From your iPad's Home screen, tap Settings, which is housed in your dock by default, then tap on Notifications, which should be the third option down on the list.

02 Add items
In Settings, you can choose which apps are featured in Notification Center. Tap Edit, then hold the right-hand edge of each app strip, and drag it into position.

03 Tailor notification options
Tap the arrow next to an app, and you will see options that are specific to that app. Choose how many items related to that app are displayed when a notification relating to it arrives.

Setting up your Notification Center

Tailoring the news feed that is all about you

Switch on
To get alerts for particular apps, ensure that the Notification Center slider is switch to On in each app you wish to see featured

Alert Style
You can decide how alerts are conveyed to you; either by the standard-style Alert, via a non-intrusive Banner, or no notifications at all

View in Lock Screen
This option determines if alerts appear on your device's Lock Screen. It is good to have this activated so that you never miss a thing

Badge icons
This slider will determine whether the icon for the app that is notifying you is displayed in the alert. It looks better if they are on

Sorting your apps
You can sort your apps on the Notification Center Settings screen by Time or Manually. Sorting by Time means that the order of alerts is based on the time they arrive. You can manually arrange the order of your Notifications by tapping Edit and then rearranging the apps by dragging them.

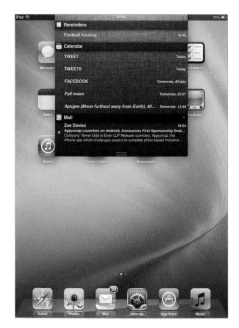

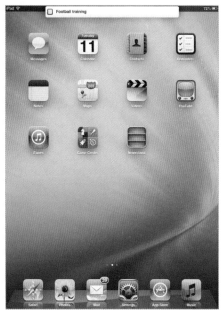

04 Access Notification Center
All you need to do is swipe down from the top of the screen to call up a window of notifications based on the options you have selected. If you liked the old boxes, you can select this option.

05 Your alerts
Notifications arrive in the form of a message at the top of the screen, and don't intrude with the app you are currently using, giving you the option to ignore it if you so wish.

06 Go to app
If you need to respond to a notification immediately, tap it in your Notification Center, and you will be taken to the specific app to carry out your actions.

App used:
FaceTime

Time needed:
10 minutes

Manage your contacts in FaceTime

If you want to make a call you have to know how to access your contacts. Here's how to add new details and delete others while managing your FaceTime contacts

The first time you use FaceTime it might be surprising to see that the Contacts section is fully populated. It's because FaceTime uses the details in the Contacts app and this in turn can import all the contacts that you have in Outlook or your Mac's Contacts. Each time there's a sync with iTunes, the contacts are synchronised across all the apps. If you don't use Outlook or Contacts then – of course – the people in the Contacts folder will just be the ones you've added.

It isn't necessary to add or delete anything using FaceTime; you can do it in the Contacts app. As soon as anything is changed here it is reflected in the FaceTime app. Any changes will then be propagated back to the desktop program you are syncing contacts with to ensure conformity across all the software. Equally, any change to a contact in FaceTime is reflected in Contacts and then transferred back when syncing. In this tutorial though, we're going to import contacts from Outlook and manage them from within FaceTime.

"FaceTime can import all the contacts that you have in Outlook or Contacts"

FaceTime Managing your contacts

01 Import contacts

Go to iTunes while performing a wireless sync. Click on your device in the pane. Click Info on the menu above the main screen. Now put a tick in the box that says 'Sync Contacts with' and select Outlook. This should populate your FaceTime contacts.

02 Delete old contacts

Perform a sync to add your Outlook contacts to both Contacts and FaceTime. Tap on FaceTime and then Contacts. To delete a contact that you won't be needing any more, tap on the name of it, then Edit. Scroll to the bottom and tap Delete Contact.

Storing the details

Add images, input details or delete old contacts entirely

Add an image
To give your contacts a more visual look tap on the Add Photo button and either use the camera to take a picture or browse the Photo Library for one. You can scale the image to fit the square

Change the tune
By default, all contacts will ring you with the same built-in ringtone which is the Strum noise. However, you can change this to any of the alarm noises by tapping on Ringtone

Remove details
To change the entry for a field just tap on it and edit it. However, to remove it completely without editing or replacement, tap on the red dash by the side on any entry

Adding favourites
If you have a lot of contacts and most of them aren't on FaceTime then it makes sense to sort them out using the Favorites button. Either add people to Favorites when looking at their details, or, if looking at the Favorites list, tap on the Plus sign and scroll through the contacts list.

03 Add new contacts
To add a new contact tap on the '+' symbol, located in the top right of the FaceTime interface. Enter all the details you have to hand then click on Add Photo. Select to either take a photo or choose one from the Library. Once you've completed this click on Done.

04 Share your contacts
To share a contact with someone else, select the contact in question and then tap on Share Contact. Type in the email address of the person to share the contact with, write your message and click on Send. All the contact details will now be emailed to that person.

App used: FaceTime   **Time needed:** 10 minutes

Make calls using FaceTime

It's one of the most exciting features of the iPad; the ability to make video calls. Here's how you sign up and then call someone for a video conversation

The addition of dual cameras to the iPad 2 was one of the worst kept secrets yet most anticipated features of the device's launch. Not so much for the ability to go out and take pictures with your iPad, but for video calling and video capture and transmission.

Yes, FaceTime arrived on the iPad 2 and it had its very own app. If you're used to an iPhone where FaceTime is built in to the phone app then this is slightly different. The cameras are the same resolution, so if you think your main screen image looks soft, it's because it's being displayed at the huge iPad size, not a tiny iPod touch screen size.

The first thing you need to have in place before any calls are made is to register FaceTime using your Apple ID. This is the ID that is used by Apple and the App Store for purchases. Once the Apple ID is set up for the FaceTime account then an email address needs to be assigned to it. This is the one that you will use to call other people and that they will use to call you.

"Before any calls are made, you must register FaceTime using your Apple ID"

FaceTime Register FaceTime and make calls

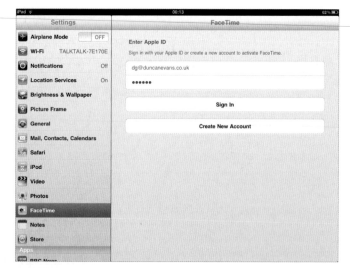

01 Register your details

To register your details, tap on the Settings app and scroll down the list of built-in apps until you get to FaceTime. Tap on this and toggle FaceTime On. You will be required to enter your Apple ID. Enter the email address and the password and then tap on Sign In to get started.

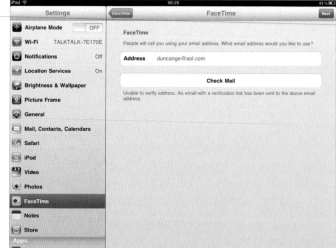

02 Select an address

FaceTime can use different email addresses. Enter the one that you would like to use for your calls. If it's the same as your Apple ID account, it will be verified immediately. However, if it is a different email address, a verification link will be sent to that address.

Making a call

It's easy to make FaceTime calls. Just find your contacts who actually use it and call away

Cameras in use
When activating FaceTime for a call, the first thing you see is yourself. When FaceTime connects the call, this window shrinks to a postage size so you can still see yourself and this main window fills with the video from the contact

Making contact
The names in this list aren't ones you've logged as FaceTime users, it's everyone in your Contacts database. Tap on a name to see if they have a FaceTime email you can use

People in touch
The list of Recent calls covers both those ringing you and you ringing them. If it's a frequent contact you want to call, it's quicker to tap here than scroll through the entire contacts list for someone's details

Dual cameras
The real advantage of having front and rear-facing cameras in a FaceTime call is that either the person calling or the one receiving, or both, can turn the other camera on and show the other person something that is going on in front of them. All you need to do is tap the camera symbol with the rotating arms to switch your camera from front facing to rear facing.

03 Get into FaceTime

Once verified, your details will be displayed and FaceTime will be on. Exit Settings and tap on the FaceTime app. This will show the display from the front-facing camera. Then simply tap on the Contacts box found at the bottom in order to list them.

04 Make a call

Tap on the person whom you would like to call. If they have a FaceTime account the email address will be shown with a blue video camera icon next to it. Tap on the email address in order to make the call. This will then telephone the contact.

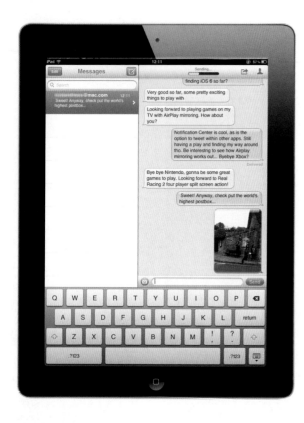

App used:
iMessage

Time needed:
5 minutes

Keep in contact with friends using iMessage

Get to grips with Apple's new messaging service and send unlimited text messages to your friends

 With iOS 6, it has never been easier to stay in touch with your friends and family using your Apple device. Thanks to iMessage, you can send unlimited text messages to everyone you know over Wi-Fi or 3G.

The app works exactly like the iPhone Messages app, letting you share photos, videos, locations and contacts around your social circles, and keep everyone in the loop via group messaging. To start, tap the 'New Message' button, and enter the mac addresses of the people you wish to contact. Then simply enter words into a text field, hitting the camera button to attach media, and tapping the Send button. The interface is fabulously intuitive. It's free, so as long as your friends have iOS 5 or iOS 6 installed, you can text without worrying about incurring a hefty bill. All messages can be tracked with delivery receipts, and thanks to the iCloud, you can start a conversation on one device, and finish it later on another. Here, we guide you through the process of using iMessage for the first time.

"It's never been easier to stay in touch with your friends and family"

iMessage How to text for free

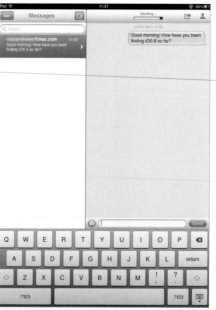

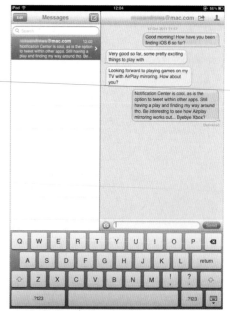

01 Create a message

To kick things off you will need to tap the 'New Message' icon, and you'll be prompted to enter the mac address of the person you wish to send a message to.

02 Type and send

Tap on the text field, and type your message into the window. When you have finished writing what you wish to say, hit Send, and your message will be delivered.

03 Quick conversations

The conversations will be neatly displayed in the main window, and the text will be colour-coded so you know who said what – blue will be your message and grey the recipient.

Free and easy messaging

Quickly conversing has never been so easy

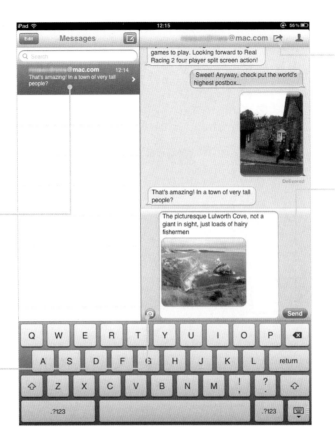

Your recipients
All of your friends will be listed in the column to the left of the window. You can bring in more people for group conversations

Adding photos
Images and videos can be added and attached to your messages. Just type your message, and then tap the camera icon to select and send media

Delete messages
Delete messages by tapping the arrow icon at the top of the window and then individually selecting messages to erase

Instant messaging
Sending messages is easy; just tap on the text field, type what you want, and hit the Send button. Each text bubble is colour-coded to make it easy to see who said what

Adding contacts
All of your Apple apps work well together. You can add contacts from iMessage to your Contacts app by tapping on the portrait icon at the top of the screen while in iMessage, and then entering the person's details into the contact page that appears.

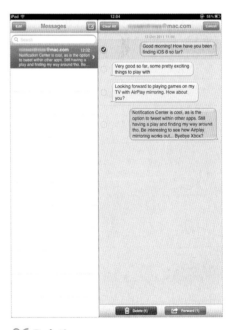

04 Add images
Once you have typed your message, tap the camera icon, pick a photograph you wish to send from your Camera Roll, and then tap Use to include it in your next message.

05 Notifications
iMessage works alongside your Notification Center, so if you receive any new messages you will be instantly notified and can then be taken straight to the app to reply.

06 Deleting messages
If there are parts of conversations you want to delete, tap the arrow in the top-right corner, and tick the circle next to the message. This will help you keep track of the important parts.

App used: Notes **Time needed:** 5 minutes

Make notes on your iPad

Don't feel you need to purchase Pages in order to jot down ideas on your iPad – you can do this just as easily with the built-in Notes app

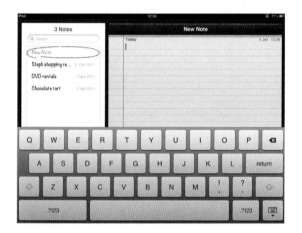

Despite the fact that some people view the iPad as a device designed merely to consume media, just spending a few minutes with it will make you realise that this isn't true. With the help of a few choice programs, the iPad is capable of being used to create drawings, edit photos or write essays. But you don't need to purchase anything for the latter, as the Notes app comes bundled with the iPad and is a really great place to start exploring how you can handle typing on glass.

Notes is remarkably similar to the program bearing the same name on the iPhone and iPod touch, it has simply been expanded a little to take advantage of the additional space the iPad screen provides. This step-by-step tutorial will show you how it works, what you can do with it, and how it could help you in your day-to-day activities.

"Notes comes bundled with the iPad and is a great place to start exploring how you can handle typing on glass"

Notes app on iPad

The Notes app is great for jotting down ideas on the go, and even copying text from the web to read later

Swipe
You don't have to select a note to delete it, just swipe its title to reveal this Delete button – just like the messages in Mail

Add
You can add as many notes as you need. Whether you're in the landscape or portrait orientation, this button is always top-right of the screen

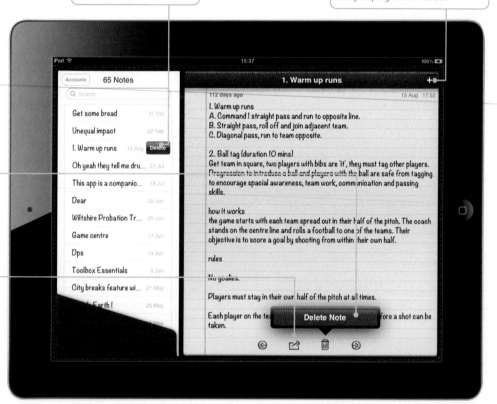

Delete
If you no longer need a particular note, select it and tap on this button. You'll be asked to confirm your choice just in case you tapped on it by mistake

Emailing
Notes lets you email the content of your pages without you having to copy and paste the information yourself. Tap on this icon to create an email message

Text, but no images
You could use Notes to keep information from the web so you can read it when you don't have access to Wi-Fi. The iPad's copy and paste system works perfectly for this, but be aware that it only lets you copy text – you can't add images to Notes.

Notes Use Notes to write down ideas

01 The look of Notes

Hold your iPad in the portrait orientation and tap the Notes app. Tap on the screen to reveal the keyboard. Now you can begin typing your very first note.

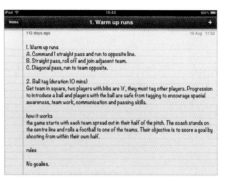

02 The '+' button

When you have finished, tap on the keyboard symbol with the down arrow (bottom-right of the keyboard) to dismiss it, then tap on the '+' button in the top-right of the interface.

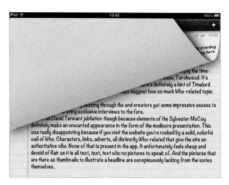

03 From one to another

That last action created a brand-new note. You can swap between the first one and the one you're currently working on by tapping on the arrow buttons.

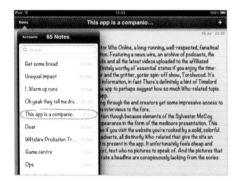

04 Pop-up menu

If you want to see all the pages you have created, tap on the Notes button to reveal a pop-up menu. They are presented in the chronological order you created them.

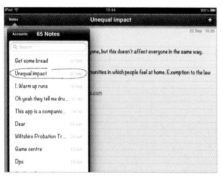

05 The selected note

Whichever note is currently selected has a big red circle around its title. You can swipe down to reveal more notes, if you have them stored on your device.

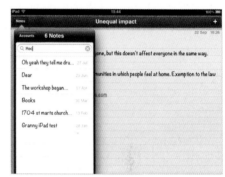

06 Searching

There's also a search field at the very top of the pop-up menu, which can help you narrow down your search when you happen to be looking for any specific information.

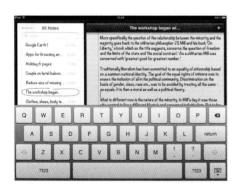

07 Landscape

Turn the iPad to the landscape orientation. The notes don't get any wider, but your list becomes permanently available on the left-hand side for easy accessibility.

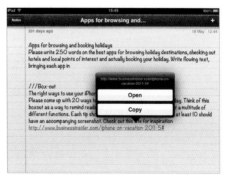

08 Tappable links

If you type in a web link, it'll become active as soon as you hide the keyboard. Tap on it and you'll be sent to Safari. Tapping an email address sends you to Mail.

09 Save numbers

Your iPad also recognises phone numbers. Since you can't phone people, you're offered two other options: to Create New Contact or Add To Existing Contact. For places you can Open in Maps.

 App used:
Maps

 Time needed:
5 minutes

Get to know the Maps app in iOS 6

Everything you need to know about the fresh new face of the Maps app for iPad in iOS 6

Ever since the iPhone and the iPad first launched, Google has provided the mapping experience on iOS. Now, with the release of iOS 6, Apple has struck out on its own and created an app from the ground up. They started completely from scratch when they began designing the app, and along with data from Yelp and TomTom, they've created a beautiful application with some amazing features.

Maps now includes turn-by-turn navigation, effectively transforming your device into a satellite navigation system. With a 3D view and Siri integration on the new iPad, you can simply tell it where you want to go and hear the instructions read back to you.

The new app also includes a 3D view for major cities around the world; when you're viewing a city in the top-down view, dragging two fingers upwards will allow you to fly through the city and pan around in 3D. We've taken a look at all the brilliant new features below, so read on to find out more about this fantastic new app.

"Apple has struck out on its own and created Maps from the ground up"

Maps The iOS 6 Maps app

Information
With the help of Yelp, there are now over 100 million added points of interest around the world – tap one and this beautiful window will appear showing information and options.

Directions
In the top-left of the screen is the Directions button. Tap it and you can get directions instantly – if you're using an iPad 3 you will get a satnav-style 3D view.

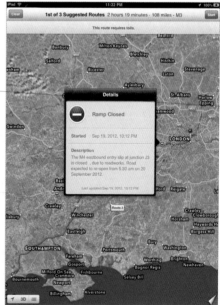

Traffic
The TomTom data also includes updates on any traffic problems. Tap an icon and you can view the time and details for each hold-up, enabling you to plan your journey around it.

The new Maps interface

It's Maps, but not as we know it

Re-aligned
If you rotate the map with two fingers, you can realign the map to face north by tapping the compass icon in the top-right of the map

3D mode
To move into 3D mode you can either drag two fingers upwards to change the angle, or tap the 3D button in the bottom-left to change it automatically

View options
Tap the fold in the bottom-right and you will see more options. You can view the map in different ways or show or hide traffic

Location data
The app still allows you to find your current location using the button in the bottom-left, with your location shown as a blue dot

Always developing
The Maps app is still in early development with Apple. While there are some features that are missing, and locations that can't be found through a search, the whole maps database will only improve in coming years. It's in constant development, and there's plenty more to come.

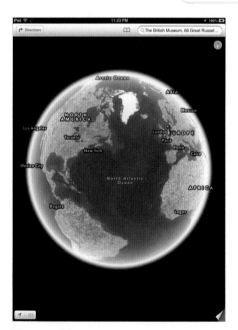

The world
The new Maps app isn't a simple flat grid like on the previous Google Maps for iPad. Zoom further out to see the entire globe and drag it around to discover place after place.

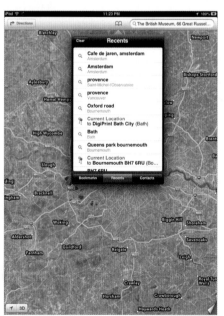

Bookmarks
Just like in Google Maps, your recent searches will be saved to the app's Bookmarks menu. You can also find your contacts and bookmarked locations included here.

Rotation
Unlike Google Maps, the new Maps app lets you use two fingers to twist the map around. This is perfect if you're following directions or need to get your bearings.

App used:
Maps

Time needed:
10 minutes

Get directions using Maps

One of the most prominent features of the Maps application is directions. You can get directions between any two locations or nearby places with a few simple taps

The Maps application on the iPad is more usable than it is on the smaller devices as there's a lot less scrolling involved. Things like Traffic and Street View look brilliant on the larger screen, and Maps also has a new Terrain view that adds a layer of topographical data to the maps.

Maps on the iPad can be used to get directions between two places. It pulls out a lot of useful information related to a route that is very useful for a commuter, such as Driving/Transit/Walking Directions, Distance and Time to Commute. When using Transit Directions it also shows you the Transit Timings to help you plan ahead. You can also make use of the Traffic information when using directions, which will help you avoid unwanted delays. Google Street View gives a panoramic view of the destination, but note that this is not available on all the locations. The locations where it is available are indicated by the Street View icon. Follow our tutorial to discover just how easy it is to get directions on your iPad and follow them with no hassle at all.

"Things like Traffic and Street View look brilliant on the larger screen"

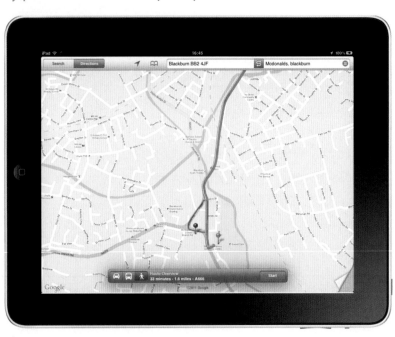

Maps Get directions using Maps

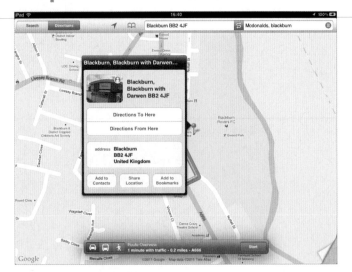

01 Set the Start Address

Search for a location on the map or, if you want to start from the current location, tap the My Location button in the bottom-left of the screen. Tap the pin to bring up the pop-up menu, and choose Directions From Here. Tap Directions, then enter the address. Now tap Search.

02 Set the destination address

Enter the destination in the End box. If there are multiple addresses, Maps will put red pins for all the searched locations. The green pin is connected by a blue line to a red pin. The green pin represents your start location, the blue line represents the route and the red pin represents the destination.

Get directions on your iPad
Use the Maps app to reach your destination

Current location
Locate the current address with the help of any of the available GPS technologies

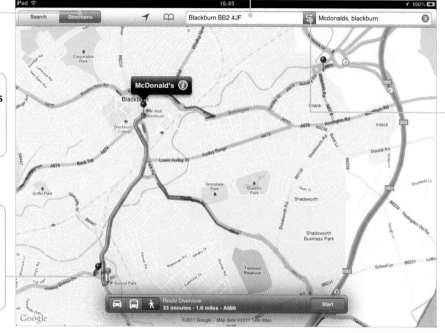

Bookmarks/ Recents/Contacts
Access Map Bookmarks, Recent Location Searches and Contacts here

Reverse directions
Reverse the searched route by simply tapping the wiggly arrow icon between the two locations

Start and destination locations
Green pins represent the start locations and red pins represent the destinations

GPS technology on iPad Wi-Fi and 3G
iPad Wi-Fi is an inferior GPS device when compared to iPad 3G. Wi-Fi depends on Skyhook Wireless Wi-Fi-based GPS technology to provide basic location specific data. Therefore it cannot be used where accurate GPS data is required. iPad 3G uses GSM and A-GPS in addition to Skyhook Wireless to determine location-specific information instead.

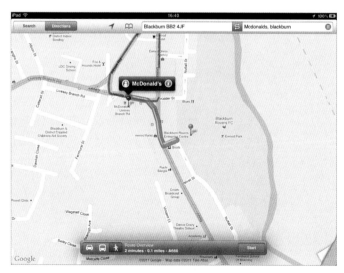

03 Get the directions
Select the method of commute by tapping one of the icons in the top left-hand corner of the map. The options are for road, public transport or on foot. When a method is selected, the route map, the applicable distance and the expected time to reach your destination will be updated automatically.

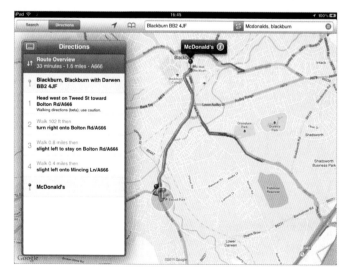

04 View turn-by-turn directions
Tap Start to view the turn-by-turn directions. Upon tapping Start you will get the driving directions on the blue bar. You can navigate through turn-by-turn directions using a swipe of a finger. Directions will indicate turns and distances so you can be sure you get the right one each time.

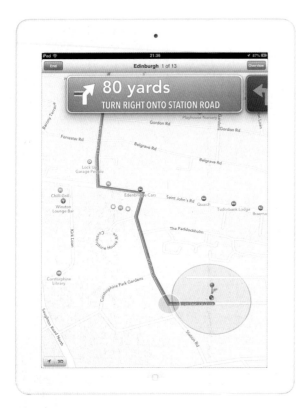

App used: Maps

Time needed: 5 minutes

Use turn-by-turn navigation in Maps

Apple's Maps is a great way to get from A to B, without having to take your eyes off the road

Maps are vital when it comes to finding your way around a strange town. But it's harder when you're finding your way around in a car. Unless you have a navigator next to you, reading a map can be a very dangerous activity.

This fact makes Apple's Maps app, which offers spoken turn-by-turn navigation, a huge boon. Set a departure point before you travel – Maps can even work out your current location – and a destination, and Maps will work out the most efficient way of getting you there. The app plots your progress to provide spoken and visual instructions as you go along the route. Your route will continue to be tracked even if you open another app, and it still works on the iPad's lock screen.

While turn-by-turn directions only come on iPad 2 or later, equipped with 3G services, Maps is still useful in these circumstances. It will still track your location and provide on-screen directions without the audio announcements.

"Unless you have a navigator, reading a map can be a very dangerous activity"

Maps Planning the best route

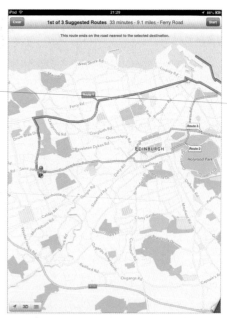

01 Choose your transport

Open the Maps app and tap the Directions button at the top-left of the screen. In the pop-up window, choose your mode of transport – pick car, walking or bus.

02 Get your directions

Choose your journey's start and end points. You will have the option to select recent locations that you have entered into Maps, and choose your current location.

03 Plan the route

Tap the Route button and Maps calculates the quickest route for you. Often the app will give you a choice between two or more routes and you can select which one you want to take.

Travels with your iPad
Get from A to B with Maps

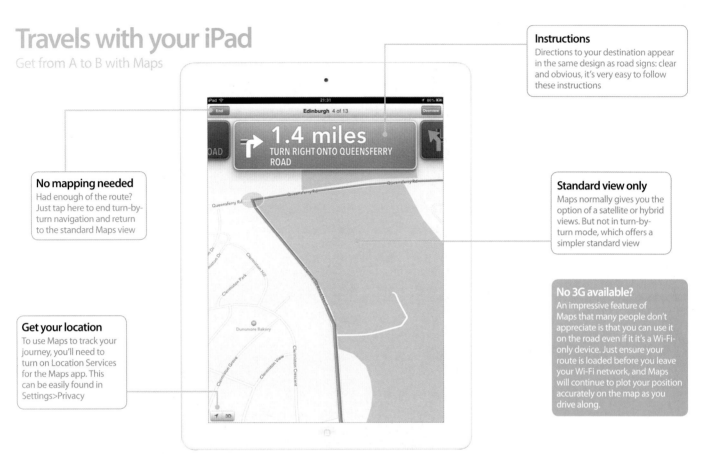

Instructions
Directions to your destination appear in the same design as road signs: clear and obvious, it's very easy to follow these instructions

No mapping needed
Had enough of the route? Just tap here to end turn-by-turn navigation and return to the standard Maps view

Standard view only
Maps normally gives you the option of a satellite or hybrid views. But not in turn-by-turn mode, which offers a simpler standard view

No 3G available?
An impressive feature of Maps that many people don't appreciate is that you can use it on the road even if it it's a Wi-Fi-only device. Just ensure your route is loaded before you leave your Wi-Fi network, and Maps will continue to plot your position accurately on the map as you drive along.

Get your location
To use Maps to track your journey, you'll need to turn on Location Services for the Maps app. This can be easily found in Settings>Privacy

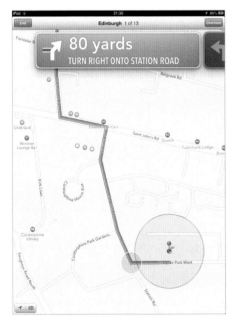

04 Turn on navigation
Tap the Start button at the top-right of the interface and Maps will display navigation instructions on screen. The app will also speak them to you.

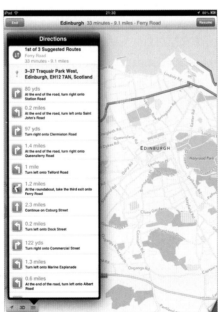

05 View listed directions
At any point you can tap the List button at the bottom of the screen. This will display a text description of your route which lists each stage of your journey.

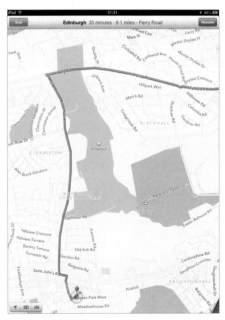

06 Overview mode
Sometimes when you're navigating, it helps to get the bigger picture: tap the Overview button to see the entire route on the screen. Tap Resume to return to the journey.

App used: Maps   **Time needed:** 5 minutes

Explore with Flyover in Maps

The new 3D mode in Maps allows you to take
a trip through the tall buildings of the city

The new Maps app is fantastic when it comes to finding your way around the major cities of the world, but what makes it truly brilliant is the new Flyover mode. It allows you to view whole cities in full 3D thanks to how Apple has photographed the buildings. They sent planes and helicopters around cities across the world to take aerial photographs of structures from every angle. Then, using complex algorithms, the images were pieced together to form 3D models of the cities that can be panned around using multi-touch gestures.

The 3D effect works even when you're viewing in top-down mode, with buildings subtly, but noticeably, changing angle as you pan across the city you're viewing. However, tap the button in the bottom-left hand corner of the screen and your view will be lowered for the full effect. The first time you do it is truly special, and it's certainly one of the best ways to show off iOS 6 to your friends. For now, though, let's take a look at how to use the new feature in the Maps application.

"Buildings subtly, but noticeably, change angle as you pan across the city"

Maps Use the new Flyover view

01 3D view

To get started with Flyover, you'll need to navigate to one of the major cities that Apple has added Flyover maps to. You can enter 3D view at any time, by tapping the button in the bottom left, but Flyover will only kick in at compatible locations.

02 Button changing

When you get close enough, the button in the bottom-left will change from displaying a 3D label to display this little icon with buildings, denoting Flyover. Tap it and your view will lower to an angle so you can see the buildings from the side. It's an incredible effect.

Fly-by
Getting to grips with Flyover

Directions
You can't use the Flyover mode in full when using turn-by-turn directions, but the 3D building data is still present in this mode. So, when you're getting directions through a city, the camera will follow your location between buildings on the screen

2D or 3D?
To move between the 3D flyover mode and the standard top-down view, you can either tap the button in the bottom-left of the screen, or simply use two fingers to alter the angle of view until you're looking straight down on the map

Always 3D
If you're in a city that is Flyover-ready, the 3D effect will always be activated. Even in top-down view, the buildings are rendered in 3D so they have height on the map. Zoom in and pan around to get an amazing effect

Location tags
The various tags that litter the map can still be easily accessed while you are in Flyover mode. Simply tap one and the preview window will appear, allowing you to view information, reviews and photos of the landmark you have selected

Multi-touch
The key to navigating around the 3D world is through multi-touch inputs on the iPad's screen. Dragging two fingers up and down the screen will change the angle at which you're viewing the earth; dragging up will bring you closer to the surface so you can see further into the distance. Twisting, pinching and two-finger scrolling are all just as important, too; this is what you will use to move around the map while in Flyover. Thankfully, every aspect of navigation feels incredibly natural, so there are no confusing moments as you try to work out what you need to do.

03 Details, details
The detail in these aerial shots is really impressive – even zoomed in to the closest levels you will be able to make out a great deal. You can pinch to zoom, twist with two fingers to rotate, and drag two fingers up or down the screen to alter the viewing angle.

04 Landscaping
Areas outside of the city aren't mapped in full flyover mode, but that doesn't mean they don't have 3D effects. Here, the cliffs by the beach have been given a gradient as they drop towards the sand; the buildings won't pop up, but the landscape's contours are incredibly accurate.

Getting started

Use Siri on your iPad

iOS 6 has brought all of the benefits of Siri to the new iPad, and it's surprisingly useful

Apple's decision to bring Siri to the new iPad was initially greeted with scepticism by those who could not see a use for such a feature on a tablet. However, the advantages do become clear the moment you start to use it. The fact that Siri has now been improved beyond recognition from the first version is the main advantage and you can now ask Siri for help with a multitude of tasks, from the everyday to the rather more obscure.

From checking local movies and when they are playing to finding all manner of local establishments, it is all there, and the process to use these features is exceptionally simple. Siri even has something of a sense of humour, as you will find out if you ask Siri what it looks like, or enquire as to the meaning of life.

The only oddity in Siri implementation on the iPad is that it uses little of the available screen space which at first appears to be an oversight. Also, when you undertake multiple searches and tasks, the limited space means you can only see some of them at any one time, but you can see everything happening in the background while you are using it.

Despite initial criticisms, Siri is definitely here to stay on the iPad. Read on to find out why this is such a good thing.

"The advantages of using Siri on an iPad become clear the moment you start using it"

Siri Get to grips with Siri

01 Activate Siri

To launch Siri all you need to do is hold down the home button and it will pop up. You will hear a beep and the microphone will turn purple which is your indicator to start speaking. Notice how it takes up very little space on the main screen.

02 Ask a question

You can now ask Siri any question you like. If you have waited a while, tap the microphone and ask your question. The answer can come back in different forms depending on what you asked, but for reference questions, they usually come back visually via WolframAlpha.

Siri's simplistic interface
The visual and audible features

Your details
Siri works best if it knows your personal details and these will come in handy time and time again. You could say 'Take me home' and the Maps app will know where that is. You can also call relatives simply by stating their relationship to you

Playing with apps
You can give instructions to Siri to set reminders, make calendar appointments, and also open apps audibly. For example you can say 'Set a reminder to pick up milk at 10am tomorrow' and Siri will create it for you

Be completely natural
You can ask Siri questions in just the same way you would with another person. The software has been designed to understand the vagaries of language and feels much less computerised than many other voice recognition solutions

Clever answers
The answers can be spoken to you by Siri or presented in a manner that fits the subject matter perfectly. For example, football scores are displayed as they would be on TV while movie times have a cinematic feel to them

Near-perfect dictation
The Siri software is also used to let you dictate long emails or anything that takes too long to type on the touch-screen keyboard. If you are in an email, you can tap the microphone on the keyboard and the familiar Siri microphone will pop up. All you have to do now is speak the words you want to write. Remember to say the punctuation and Siri will do the rest for you. It has been proven that the more you use the system, the more accurate it gets and in tests we have been able to achieve great speeds.

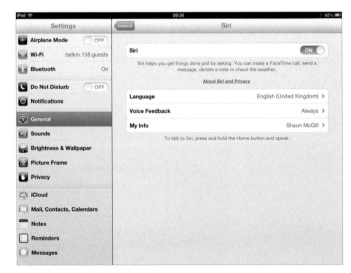

03 Siri settings
In Settings>General>Siri you can choose whether to activate the service or not and to specify your language as well. The 'My Info' section is important and you should make sure that you have a contact set up for yourself with all of your relevant information detailed.

04 Add relationships
If you have contacts for your partner, children, and so on, it is worth telling Siri how these relate to you. Once you have, you can say things like "Message my wife" in the future and Siri will know exactly who to contact. It makes communicating from your iPad much quicker.

App used:
Siri

Time needed:
15 minutes

Master Siri's new iOS 6 features

Siri in iOS 6 is so different to the solution built in to iOS 5 that it can now answer almost anything

Siri was initially designed to be a personal assistant that could answer all of your questions and perform tasks for you by simply understanding what you said to it. However, the original version was cut down to the point that many people found it hard to use, difficult to connect to at times and limited in scope. The latest version changes all of this and you can now use voice to search, contact people and also control many aspects of your iPad.

In this tutorial we will highlight the latest features and also show you how to make the most of them. As with all things, you need to consider if Siri is the best option for every task you want to perform, but the more you use it, the more useful it becomes. Its transition to the iPad has also proved successful and despite not having an obvious place on a tablet, it surely does work as well as you could hope for. Siri is now the personal assistant you always dreamed of without the expense of a salary.

"Siri is now the personal assistant you always dreamed of without the expense of a salary"

Siri Understanding the advanced features

All the sports

Sports results are now offered by Siri and you can check up on the latest scores anytime. Simply ask a question, making sure to include the specific team name or sport.

Find local establishments

No matter what you need that's local to you, just ask. You could say "I want to get a coffee" and the answers will appear immediately, offering a range of places that are suitable based on location.

Points of interest

You can now ask Siri to show you a particular place or building, and it will pop up a map and show how far away it is to wherever Siri currently registers that you are.

The beautiful Siri interface

An intuitive and
responsive design

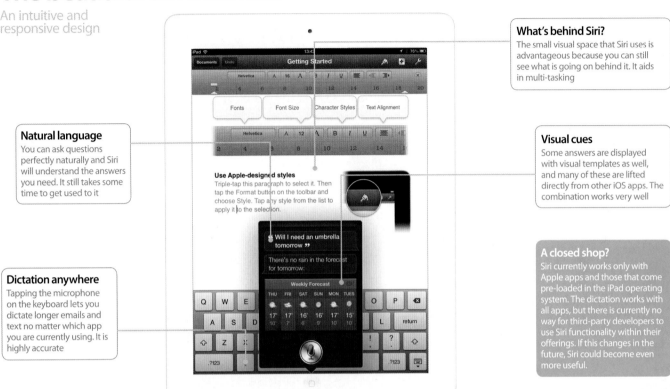

What's behind Siri?
The small visual space that Siri uses is advantageous because you can still see what is going on behind it. It aids in multi-tasking

Natural language
You can ask questions perfectly naturally and Siri will understand the answers you need. It still takes some time to get used to it

Visual cues
Some answers are displayed with visual templates as well, and many of these are lifted directly from other iOS apps. The combination works very well

Dictation anywhere
Tapping the microphone on the keyboard lets you dictate longer emails and text no matter which app you are currently using. It is highly accurate

A closed shop?
Siri currently works only with Apple apps and those that come pre-loaded in the iPad operating system. The dictation works with all apps, but there is currently no way for third-party developers to use Siri functionality within their offerings. If this changes in the future, Siri could become even more useful.

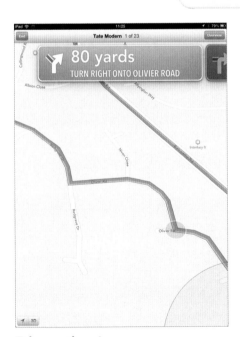

Take me there!

Once a location has been found, simply say "Take me there" and the Maps app will appear, ready to navigate you to your chosen destination with comprehensive instructions.

Control your apps

You can now open apps in Siri by saying "Open…" followed by the app name. This is surprisingly quicker than using the Spotlight search feature.

Incredibly quick notes

Adding notes is now also much easier, thanks to Siri. You can say "Note…" followed by the note text and it will be added to the Notes app. Couldn't be simpler!

App used:
App Store

Time needed:
20 minutes

Explore the new App Store

The iPad's App Store underwent an exciting revamp as part of iOS 6

As part of the huge iOS 6 update that launched in the autumn of 2012, all Apple mobile stores received a **substantial make-over.** The new App Store has been completely overhauled in order to produce a more efficient user experience, and it has certainly succeeded. The App Store on your iPad is now easier than ever to navigate.

Of the new features, perhaps the most significant is being able to download new apps inside the App Store, rather than being taken to one of your homepages. There's also a new intuitive Genius bar to give you clever recommendations.

Other new features include being able to view each app's update history, as well as individual developer pages. Facebook integration is also present, while the ability to view app screenshots in full screen is a big positive.

This is definitely not an upgrade to worry about, but one to embrace. All your favourite options remain, but most have received a little bit of Apple's magic dust. Let's have a closer look at four of the most important changes.

"The App Store on your iPad is now easier than ever to navigate"

App Store So what's new?

Stay put

The biggest change to the App Store is based on purchasing new apps. Instead of being whisked away to your homescreen from the app when you hit the buy button, you can now watch the installation process inside the App Store itself. It's a welcome addition!

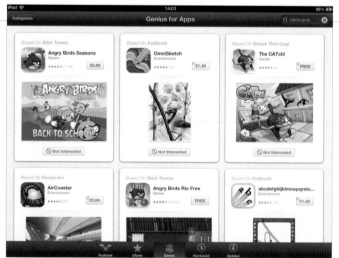

Genius tab

The App Store now provides a Genius tab to recommend apps based on your previous purchases. Hit Genius at the bottom of the main screen, enter your Apple ID and agree to the terms. Now when you hit Genius again, you'll be presented with a screen of apps specific to you.

Top Charts
Downloading your first apps

Number one
You can vertically swipe through three different fields in a chosen category: Paid, Free and Top Grossing. Each list contains the top 100 apps in that category, showcasing the very best the App Store has to offer

Categories
Within the Chart interface, you'll find an All Categories tab in the top-left. This gives you the option to flick through different categories. There are 24 categories in total, so you're bound to discover something of interest

Search
If you can't find exactly what you're looking for, then there's always the manual search bar situated in the top-right of the screen to fall back on. As you type into the search, live results will appear below

Installing
If you find the app you're looking for, you can download it right there and then thanks to a new iOS 6 feature. After installing you'll be presented with an Open button, which will take you directly to the app. It's just so simple!

Facebook integration
As part of the system-wide integration of social-networking giant Facebook in iOS 6, you now have the ability to 'like' an app. If you do so, the action will appear on your News Feed for all your friends to see. If you wish to leave a bit more detail about your app experience, you still have the chance to do so as normal. You can rate each app out of five stars and leave your own comment for other users and developers.

Revamped UI
The new-style App Store has been built from the ground up. It's a comprehensive re-design that ultimately makes it easier than ever before to navigate. Menus can be intelligently swiped through, and it all looks perfect on the large real estate your iPad provides.

Sharing options
If you come across an app you're fond of, or one that you think everyone needs to know about, however well known, iOS 6 has added a selection of sharing options for you to utilise. Simply hit the share icon to view your different options.

App used:
iTunes

Time needed:
10 minutes

Explore the new iTunes app

Making purchases has never been so easy

Much the same as the App Store, the iTunes Store has undergone a major design overhaul. Your iPad's screen size showcases the re-design perfectly. The added screen real estate is unbeatable. When you open up the new app, you will instantly be greeted by the latest and most popular options. New releases are showcased at the top and you now have the ability to browse with a swipe of your finger.

Of course, further iCloud integration ensures all your past purchases are up to date. You can start shopping on your iPhone and seamlessly check out over on your iPad. As part of the iOS 6 update, you can download songs, albums and films from iTunes without leaving the app. Instead of being frogmarched to your Downloads tab, you can now view a download's progress via a handy in-app status bar. It's all part of making the buying process simpler than ever.

All the usual features remain untouched. This update is only a cosmetic one, but one that we're sure provides a much more intuitive user experience. Here's a quick overview of the features you need to know about.

"You can now view a download's progress via a handy in-app status bar"

iTunes Shop 'til you drop

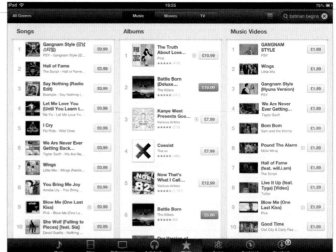

Homepages

The first time you load the app, it will appear very different. Lots has changed, but it's all for the better. There are homepages for Music, Films, TV Programmes and Audiobooks, and you can swipe through popular categories like top singles, albums and new releases.

Charts

Each category has its most popular downloads listed under the Charts tab that you can find at the bottom of the app highlighted by a star symbol. The music section, for example, lets you vertically scroll through the top 100 songs, albums and music videos. Everything is at your fingertips.

Become an iTunes expert

Find your way around the new interface

Search

Sometimes, whatever it is that you're looking for won't be part of the latest charts or a new release. iTunes has you covered via an excellent search facility. Start typing in what you're looking for and live results will appear below

Big banners

New releases and big sellers now take pride of place in the iTunes app through a running series of big banners at the top of the app. Tap on one for extra information or to buy. Record companies will be desperate to get this sort of publicity!

Genius

Because all your previous purchases are linked to your Apple ID, the Genius tab acts as a personal shopper based on what you've bought. You'll be surprised at just how effective it can be

Downloads

As soon as you hit the Buy button, your purchase will begin downloading. You can keep track of its progress from within the Download menu – especially good if you want to check how long a feature-length film has left before the end

History

New to iOS 6 is a history button that lets you keep track of all the films, TV programmes and music you've been previewing in the iTunes app. That goes for any device, too. With iCloud integration now baked into Apple's mobile operating system, your history will be instantly available on any iOS device you have linked to your all-important Apple ID. It's never been easier to get your hands on great entertainment. Preview a movie on your journey home from work, then download it your iPad back in the comfort of your own home.

Extra info

If you find something that you're interested in, a straightforward tap on its title will take you to a page packed with extra information. Do so with a film, and you'll find details such as trailers, ratings and reviews, and you'll have the ability to buy it by tapping its price.

Previous purchases

Since the introduction of iCloud, all your pre-iCloud purchases can be viewed and downloaded on multiple devices. Hit the Purchased tab and use the 'Not on this iPad' option to search for songs or an artist. If there's something you want to download, all you've got to do is tap the cloud icon next to it.

Getting started

App used: iTunes

Time needed: 10 minutes

Use iTunes to download media

We show you how to use Apple's virtual superstore to purchase music, films and other assorted media

The birth of iTunes signalled a significant change in the way we shop for music and media. Everything can now be bought whenever and wherever we are and it's all thanks to iTunes.

The iTunes app for your iPad is a friendly and welcoming portal to a thriving online marketplace where you can shop at your leisure and not be suckered into slinging cheap tat that is on display next to the tills into your basket. You go in, get what you want and, within minutes, be listening to it through your iPad's Music app or watching it through the Videos app. Using iTunes really couldn't be easier. Everything is well laid out and easily accessible and all of your past and present purchases are with you at all times for when you need them. The hardest part, if there even is a hard part, is ensuring that all of your billing information is up-to-date and correct. Once it is, all of the sonics and flicks you could ever want will be at your fingertips. Here we guide you through this essential app.

"iTunes is a friendly and welcoming portal to a thriving online marketplace"

iTunes How to browse and buy media

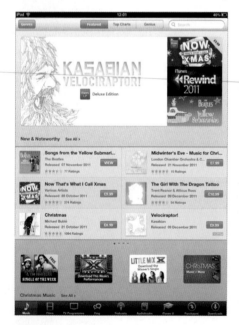

01 Launch iTunes

When you launch the iTunes app you will be taken straight to the main storefront, which is the Music Store by default. All of the categories in the store are laid out across the bottom of the screen.

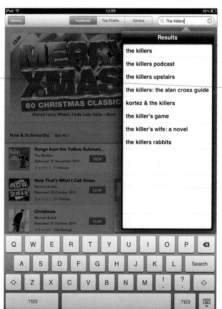

02 Browse the store

The newest, most exciting media will always be displayed on the main page. If you don't find what you want there then you can search for artists and albums by using the 'Search' window.

03 Purchase music

When you find what you want, tap on it to bring up a window. Then tap the price at the top to buy the entire album, or tap on the price next to the separate tracks to download them individually.

Exploring the iTunes app

Navigating the user-friendly interface

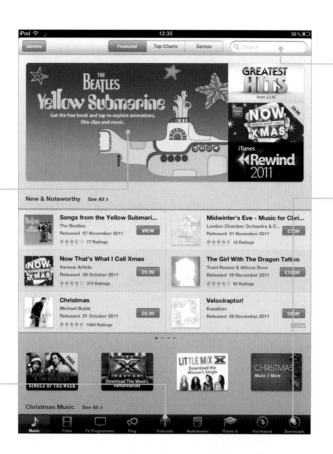

Search for content
You can use the 'Featured', 'Top Charts' and 'Genius' tabs to find media, or you can enter specific keywords into the Search engine to instantly find what you want

Featured content
All of the most recent, hottest releases will be displayed in the main 'Featured' window that appears when you first tap on each store section

Downloads
When you purchase a song, film or other media from iTunes, they will be sent to the Downloads section where you can see their download progress by tapping on this icon here

Store categories
All of the different store categories, such as Music, Films, TV Shows, etc, are displayed as icons along the bottom of the screen. Tap on one to access it

Get past purchases
With iCloud integration, it isn't just your current purchases that are pushed to your other iOS 6 devices. A section in the iTunes app, called 'Purchased' will allow you to view all media downloaded through your Apple ID and allow you to instantly download it again onto your current device.

04 Authorise download
After opting to download an item you will be required to sign in using your Apple ID to authorise the purchase. You may also be required to enter billing information.

05 Buy more media
You can also purchase films, TV shows, podcasts, audiobooks and educational materials through iTunes. The main difference being that with movies you can choose to rent, as well as buy.

06 iTunes in the Cloud
The iTunes app is compatible with your personal iCloud, which means that anything you purchase from the store will be automatically pushed to all of your other iOS 6 devices free of charge.

The next step

104
Use Photo Stream

130
Subscribe to magazines

142
Print from your iPad

148
Utilise Facebook

"Touch is the key word when it comes to editing projects in iMovie on your iPad, and the system works so naturally"

Get to grips with the iPad's more in-depth features with our guides

"Edit photos and share them with others"

The next step

Take faster photos on your iPad

Use the abilities of the iPad 2 and new iPad to take great photos faster using the volume button

While the iPad 2 was able to take photos from its launch, the only technique was initially a tap of the screen to take your snap. Sadly, due to the size of the device, touching the centre of the screen while holding it up is a little difficult and can lead to hand shake and motion blur in your shots. Luckily, though, there is now a way around this issue.

iOS 5 brought with it several new and useful abilities inside the Camera app, all of which make taking and viewing your photos a lot quicker and easier. By far the most useful feature, though, is the option to take a snapshot with the 'Volume Up' button on the side of your device. It's quick, easy and most of all it's comfortable to reach when holding the iPad up to take your photo, making this one of the best additions to iOS 5 that Apple has introduced, which inevitably remained in iOS 6.

However, that isn't the end of it – viewing your photos is even easier thanks to a new way to access your Camera Roll, simply by swiping across the screen. And now you can even edit your photos on the iPad as soon as you've taken them, ensuring that even a skewed shot can be straightened out, right on your iPad. In this guide we take you through all the key features iOS 5 and iOS 6 have to offer.

Camera Take incredible photos

The screen
In the Camera app, you'll see a shutter button in the centre of the bottom bar, and two buttons at the top to change the camera direction and the settings you are using.

Zoom in and out
The gesture for zooming in and out with the camera is very natural. You can pinch in and out with two fingers, just as you do to zoom in on other apps.

Video recording
You can tap the toggle at the bottom right of the screen to switch between photo and movie mode. The camera records 720p video, so it's of a good quality.

Taking a fast snapshot

Make the most of the Camera app

Volume button
Tapping the volume button on the top right of your iPad will allow you to take a photograph without even touching the screen

Options
Unlike the iPhone 4S and 5, which has an LED flash option, your choice here is limited to adding gridlines to the screen while you shoot

Tap to expose
You can tap anywhere on the screen to make a small focus square appear. It sets the focus on the item you tapped and alters the lighting of the scene

Access to library
You have the ability to access your Camera Roll without carefully tapping the icon in the bottom left. You simply need to swipe from the left

Photo editing
When you've taken a shot, you can edit the photo right on your iPad by choosing the Edit button when viewing your photos. This will give you options to Enhance, Straighten, Crop and Rotate your shot, as well as give you the chance to remove red-eye from your shots.

Gridlines
If you want to line up your shots perfectly, turn Gridlines on by tapping the Options button at the top of the screen and swiping the slider to 'On'. This will help you when composing your shots.

Face the front
The front-facing camera on the isn't just for FaceTime – it can also be used to take snapshots too. Just tap the icon in the top right of the screen and take the photo with the volume up button.

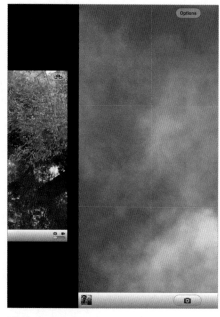

View your shots
If you tap the tiny image at the bottom left you'll view your Camera Roll, but you can also just swipe from the left edge of the screen if you want to view it quickly.

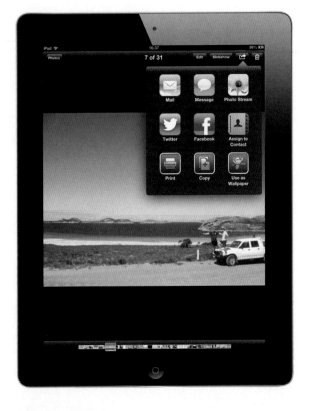

 App used:
Photos

 Time needed:
10 minutes

Edit images in Photos

Make the most of your iPad's camera, and take advantage of the built-in photo-editing feature

Since the release of iOS 5 back in 2011, you have been able to edit your images directly from the Photos app. Admittedly, the editing software isn't going to turn your photos into works of art with just a couple of taps, but it does help to enhance both photos taken with the camera and photos already on the device. iOS 6 only improves upon this.

The editing features available include the ability to rotate images from portrait to landscape. There's also an enhance option, which can adjust the colour depth, brightness and contrast, transforming a relatively dull photo into something that is altogether more pleasant to look at. The last few options should prove to be useful as well; the first of these allows you to remove the notorious red-eye that you get in dark photos overloaded with flash, and the second enables you to crop images.

For this tutorial, you will have needed to upgrade your iPad to at least iOS 5, preferably iOS 6, as not all of the features highlighted here are available with earlier operating systems. Head to the Settings app and tap General>Software Update to keep up to date.

"It isn't going to turn your photos into works of art, but it does enhance them"

Photos Edit your photographs on your iPad

01 Select your photo
Launch the Photos app from the home screen, and you will automatically see all your pictures and videos. Pick one you want to make amendments to, and then tap Edit.

02 Rotate the photo
From the Edit Photo screen, select the Rotate option at the bottom, and keep tapping this in order to rotate the orientation. Tap Save when you are done.

03 Enhance the image
If you choose Enhance, the software will adjust the colours of the image. Tap the same option again to cancel the changes, or tap Save to finish.

Editing interface

Editing your photos is as intuitive as the iPad itself

Undo any changes
Thanks to the intuitiveness of the iPad, you can easily revert back to the original image by pressing cancel, and then quickly resave it

Forward Photo
Once you have made changes to your photo, you can use the share option to assign the photo to a message, use it as your wallpaper, email, tweet or even print. iOS 6 even brings Facebook integration as an option. The Assign to Contact menu choice is also useful for adding images next to your contacts' names.

Multi-touch controls
Before you choose how to edit a photo, you can use the multi-touch pinch controls to zoom in to the photo to focus on the areas you want to improve

Enhance
On the surface this seems like a basic option compared to most dedicated editing packages, but in practice it's a great feature that can transform your photo within moments

Crop photos
Crop is another underestimated feature. You can chop out parts of the photo (such as a blurred section or distraction) that you don't want anymore

04 Remove red-eye

Select an image where people have red eyes, then tap on the Red-Eye option. Next, click on the person's eyes to remove the red. Click Save to finish.

05 Crop the photo

Select an image to edit, and from the list of options, choose Crop. Drag your finger to resize the photo, or alternatively you can tap on the Constrain option.

06 Undo changes

If you've made a mistake during the editing process, you can always choose the Cancel command at the top of the screen to leave your images untouched.

Create a slideshow

App used:
Photos

Time needed:
15 minutes

Show your best pictures off with a cool slideshow, complete with transitions and your own music

Apple has taken a lot of time over the Photos app on the iPad. We know this because it's a completely different app to the one that appears on the iPhone, even though they both share the same operating system. One of the things that sets this new Photos app apart is its ability to show incredible picture slideshows, with far more control than the iPhone equivalent. A large part of this is, of course, down to the larger screen with greater resolution, but another part is the way the interface is so easy to use that you'll really enjoy creating and watching them with friends.

Once you've learned how to create a slideshow, we're confident that you'll be so impressed that you'll be making them all the time. The real shame is that, unlike the desktop version in iPhoto, you can't save the results and share them with others. For now, though, just enjoy the brilliance of these slideshows.

"iPad's Photos can show picture slideshows with far more control than the iPhone equivalent"

Photos Setting up a slideshow

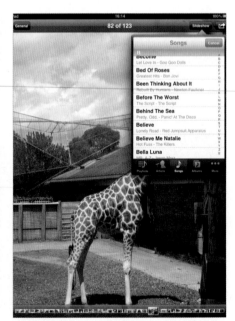

01 Load it, tap it
Load the Photos app from your home screen and then navigate to an album or a picture that you like. Then tap the 'Slideshow' button at the top of the interface to begin.

02 Options
The options window will now appear and you can begin to customise your slideshow. Tap on the transition you wish to use between photos. You have the choice of five different ones.

03 Tune it
You can add music to the slideshow by tapping the music button. This will bring up all of your songs that have been synced from iTunes, so if you want a specific song make sure it's on there.

The iPad slideshow interface

Be amazed at how simply you can create a beautiful slideshow

Transitions
Origami is a new Apple transition type and it basically looks as though photos are folding out from under each other. Very cool

Pop-ups
Having windows within windows makes navigation on the iPad a complete joy. You pretty much always stay on the same page

Rotation
As you would expect, the photos will auto-rotate when the iPad is itself rotated. This way you can get the most from both portrait and landscape pictures

Scrubber
The Photos app has a cool and very easy to use scrubber at the bottom of the interface, so you can navigate through a large number of pictures very easily

Sounds
The integration of music into the slideshow adds a whole new dimension to watching your pictures. Your music can really set the mood. It is possible to create a playlist from the Music app on the iPad, so you can create something specific on the fly.

04 Playlist it
If you are really organised you will have already created a custom playlist for the slideshow and can use this now. Tap on whatever you wish to use to select it and you're just about ready to go.

05 Ready, steady
Once you have everything in place, just tap the 'Start Slideshow' button at the bottom of the 'Slideshow Options' window. Your slideshow will begin immediately with your chosen settings.

06 Watch in awe
You can now relax with the iPad, watching your favourite pictures from your most recent holiday or event and listening to your favourite tunes while you do it. It's as simple as that.

The next step

Get started with Photo Stream

Start using iPhoto to back up and share your images across all your Apple devices

Apple introduced Photo Stream in iOS 5, and it has since seen a fantastic upgrade in iOS 6. The premise of Photo Stream is a relatively simple one – if you set it up on other devices, such as an iPhone or a Mac that is running iPhoto, you are able to view the photos that you take and add to those devices on your iPad, and vice versa.

All of these photos are stored in iCloud for free, so you'll simply need to take a snap and it will be saved immediately, and accessible everywhere. There is a limited time on these photos, so any shots taken will be removed after 30 days, and your Stream can only hold 1,000 images at once, so keeping it tidy is also very important.

In iOS 6, however, Apple has also added the ability to share Photo Streams with friends and family members. It's a quick and easy way to share your shots, and those you share with can Like and comment on your shots. So, let's get started with Photo Stream to back up and share your snapshots.

"All of your photos are stored in iCloud for free with Photo Stream"

Photo Stream Photo Stream explained

01 Find your Stream

First, open up the Photos app. Along the top of the window you will see multiple options – choose the second one, Photo Stream, to see the shots currently in your Stream.

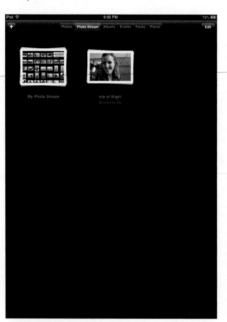

02 Multiple Streams

The first time you enter this area you will only see My Photo Stream as an option, but as you share more Streams they will appear too. For now, choose the first option.

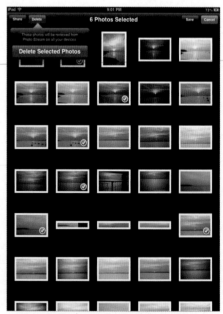

03 Clean up

If you have screenshots or duplicate images in your Photo Stream across every device, you can delete them by selecting Edit in the top-left, tapping the photos and hitting delete.

Photo Stream options

More than just a storage service

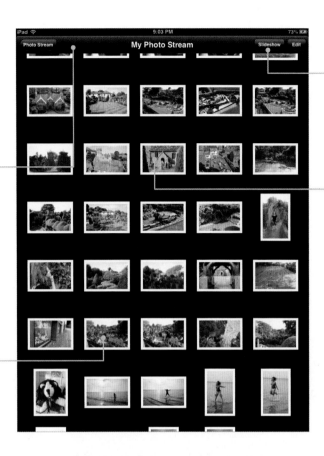

Slideshow
Tap the slideshow button in the top-right and you will be presented with options for changing the type of transitions and adding music, before hitting start

More Streams
You can view the Shared Photo Streams that you, or your friends and family, have added to the area by tapping the back arrow on this screen

High resolution
The images in your Photo Stream are downloaded at full resolution, so even if you add photos to a device from a DSLR, the quality is maintained even through Photo Stream

Deleting for good
Deleting an image from your Photo Stream will remove it from the Stream on every device you own, but won't delete the original photo – that will be stored in the Camera Roll area of the device on which it was taken.

Shared forever?
Apple haven't made clear whether photos that have been removed from your Photo Stream due to time constraints or limited numbers will still be shared, so be careful

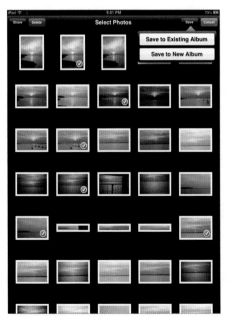

04 Save

Select multiple images and you can save them to a new or existing Album, too. If these were taken on a different device this is a great way to save the images to your iPad.

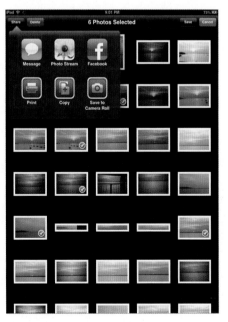

05 Share Streams

To share photos with others, choose Edit and select the images you want to share, then tap the Share button in the top-left. Choose the Photo Stream option.

06 Comment and Like

Photos shared by you or by others can be commented on and Liked by tapping the small speech bubble icon in the bottom left. Everyone in the Stream will see these comments.

App used:
Photos

Time needed:
10 minutes

Use Photo Stream to sync your photos

Take advantage of Apple's iCloud service to get your photos automatically pushed to all of your devices

One of the handiest features of iOS 6 is Photo Stream. Using your own personal iCloud, with Photo Stream activated, you can get photos transported automatically – and totally wirelessly – to all of your iOS 6/Mac OS X Mountain Lion devices on the same Wi-Fi network. So if you take a picture on your iPhone, within seconds it will appear on your iPad. If you take some snaps on your iPad then they will be beamed to your iPhone and your Mac without you having to lift a finger. The whole process eradicates the need to email individual images, or copy them onto portable storage devices to transport across to your other devices. It's a quick and convenient process that just occurs in the background.

In order to set up Photo Stream, you must first set up your iCloud account. This is a free service that replaces Apple's MobileMe service and it provides a host of great features, such as the option to sync documents and files, music, bookmarks, contact details and calendar events across all of your devices, as well as backing up your important data. Setting up iCloud is easy: you go to Settings, tap on the 'iCloud' section and then log in with your standard Apple ID (the same email address and password that you use for your other Apple services, such as the App Store and iTunes). In this tutorial we guide you through the process.

Photos How to activate your Photo Stream

01 Update to iOS 5 or iOS 6

Photo Stream is a service that comes as part of the iOS 5 or iOS 6 operating system, so connect your device to your computer through iTunes and ensure that you have the latest free software update installed on your device.

02 Activate your iCloud

With iOS 6 installed, go to Settings>iCloud and then activate your free iCloud account by logging in with your Apple ID (the same email address and password that you use to log in to the other Apple services).

03 Turn on Photo Stream

You have full freedom of which iCloud services you use and you can toggle them on or off from Settings>iCloud. Included in the list of compatible apps is 'Photo Stream', so move the slider to 'On' to activate it.

Your synced photos

Thanks to Photo Stream you need never manually transfer your photos again

Easy sharing
Once your images are in your Photos app, you can then easily share them with others via email, tweeting, attaching them to an SMS text message and more

Tap, pinch, expand
All images that are automatically imported into your Photo Stream album can be tapped on, expanded and pinched to shrink like normal through your Photos app

Photo Stream
Once activated, Photo Stream will automatically update your Photos app with all of the images captured on other devices, wirelessly. Impressive, huh?

Your photos
Your Photo Stream album will be updated as and when new images are captured on other devices linked to your iCloud. Take pictures, sit back and watch the magic happen

All cameras supported
Photo Stream isn't restricted to iDevices. If you plug a non-Apple digital camera into your Mac (which is running at least Mac OS X 10.7.2 with iCloud enabled), all of the images on that camera will also be automatically whipped off and pushed straight to your Photo Stream too. Now that really is impressive.

04 Take pictures

To discover the magic of Photo Stream, follow the previous steps on your iPhone device and then start taking photos. Within a minute, open up the Photos app on your iPad and then tap on the new 'Photo Stream' tab.

05 Instant transferal

As if by magic, all of the photos that you have taken on your iPhone will start appearing in your Photo Stream album, completely doing away with the need to manually transfer images by email or actually copying them across.

06 View and edit

You now have complete access to all of the photos taken on all of your devices and can go about editing them and sharing them with others – it's a great, seamless system that will save you hours of time and effort in the long run.

The next step

 App used:
Photos

 Time needed:
20 minutes

Create a Photo Stream web album

Create an amazing web album to share with your friends and view it from anywhere

With iOS 5 last year, Apple updated the iPad to utilise Photo Stream, a system that allows you to save all your latest snaps across your devices. Now, in iOS 6, this feature has been updated, allowing you to share photos in your Stream with friends and family. Shared Photo Streams allow you to quickly pick the shots you want to share, then choose the friends you want to share them with. While the system is designed to integrate with Apple devices, if your friends only own a PC, the images are still available through a special album on the internet that will be created when you share your Stream. You can choose to make this public if you wish, or simply limit it so that only your chosen friends can view them. However, all of the shots will be shared at full resolution, so whether they just want to view the shots, or if they want to save them to their own devices, the images will be downloaded at full size for the very best quality.

"You can view the photos through a special album that's created automatically on the internet"

Sharing your photo stream

The best way to share photos

Comments
Hit the Next button on this screen to add a comment to the album. Comments and likes to individual photos will be viewable by everyone in the sharing group

Public or private?
To view your shared photos from any device, you'll need the Public Website switch in the on position. If it's off, only those with iOS devices or a Mac will be able to view them

Recipients
You can share your Photo Stream with anyone in your contacts book, or simply add an email address or phone number for the person you want to show your photos to. As long as they have an email address they'll be able to view your shots online

Outside the Stream
You can only share photos that are currently in your Photo Stream with people online. If your snaps are saved in an album on your iPad, or have disappeared past the 1000 photo limit, you won't be able to share them

Photos Create a web album

01 Find your photos

First, open up the Photos app. By default you'll be taken into the Photos tab, so choose Photo Stream at the top of the screen to view the shots available through your Stream.

02 Start selecting

To start choosing photos to share, hit the Edit button in the top-right corner. Then tap the photos you want; a tick will appear next to those you have selected and a count appears at the top.

03 Share

To start Sharing your photos, tap the Share button in the top-left. You'll see a new grid layout for the sharing section; tap Photo Stream to share the photo with others quickly.

04 Choose friends

Now you'll need to pick the people you want to send your Stream to. You can tap the plus button to view your contacts, or simply start typing a name to choose a friend

05 Name the Stream

Next, choose a name for your Photo Stream. Make it something that explains what the photos are about, as the email inviting your friends to view the shots will list this as the title.

06 Make it public

You're given the choice of whether or not to make the Photo Stream public on a website, which is essential for PC users, so slide this switch to the on position to create a web album.

07 Comment

The next screen that will appear allows you to make a comment on the shared album before it is sent to your friends. It's completely optional, but a nice way to explain what the photos are about.

08 Join the Stream

Now your friends and family will receive emails telling them that there is a Photo Stream available for viewing. They can view it in the web interface by clicking the link at the bottom.

09 View and save

Now you will see the photos, set out beautifully in a grid. Click or tap one to go into a high-resolution full-screen view, and you can click to save the photos to your device.

App used:
Photo Booth

 Time needed:
5 minutes

Take photos with Photo Booth

Photo Booth is capable of applying weird and wonderful camera effects and using both the front and rear-facing cameras on your iPad. It's a bit crazy, but also tremendous fun

 Photo Booth made its debut on the Mac some years ago, when built-in iSight cameras became standard across most models of Apple computers. Now thanks to the cameras on the iPad 2 and third-generation iPad, it has made its way to the device and it's a fun way to take snapshots of yourself and your friends, or just to take strange-looking photos of anything you can point a camera at.

The app itself is a little more limited on the iPad for some reason, with fewer effects and without the ability to record video with effects, but it's still great fun to play with. The touch screen interface means that when effects have a focus point, which is to say that they distort the image based on a certain area of the screen, you can use your finger to change the position and so edit the effect. Some of the others are just on or off – they can't be edited. Of course you are also able to use either the front or rear-facing cameras depending on whether you wish to photograph yourself or someone else.

"It's certainly a fun way to take snapshots of yourself and your friends"

Photo Booth Take pictures in Photo Booth

01 Fire it up
Open Photo Booth and it should default to using the front-facing camera. You'll see a range of different crazy effects and if you tap on one, you will get to see that effect in full screen.

02 Light Tunnel
This is the Light Tunnel effect and if you drag with your finger, you will be able to position the centre of the effect over any part of the screen. This applies to other effects that distort the image.

Using Photo Booth

Use Photo Booth's wacky effects to create fun and outlandish pictures to share or use on social networking sites

Take a picture
Press the shutter button to take a snapshot and the image will be saved to a special camera roll inside Photo Booth. Form there, pictures can be deleted, viewed or emailed

The image
The weird and wonderful results of Photo Booth's effects can be seen on the main screen. This is a thermographic effect here

Camera flip
The iPad 2 and third-generation iPad have both front and rear-facing cameras and you can flip between them by using this icon. The effects all work the same way through both cameras

Effects
To return to the effects list, click the effects icon. You will be able to choose from the built-in effects such as pinch, twirl, X-ray, mirror and a host of other strange ones

Hardware requirements
The kinds of real-time image processing performed by Photo Booth actually place quite a strain on hardware, though the reason it isn't included on the iPad 1 is because it doesn't have any cameras. You're not able at present to apply Photo Booth effects to video on the iPad, though this may be something that Apple chooses to unlock with a software update at some point in the future.

03 View your pictures
Pictures that you take are shown along the bottom. Scroll around and load up any one to view it full screen. Click the camera chooser to flip to the rear camera, or the effect icon to choose a different effect.

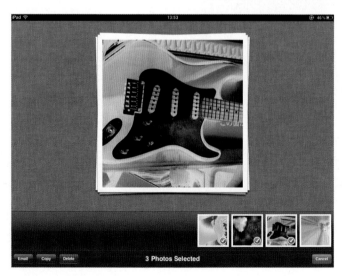

04 Share pictures
Click on the Share button and you can choose a number of pictures to either place in an email, copy, or delete. They are shown in a helpful stack view. If you deselect a picture it 'slides' out of the stack.

The next step

 App used:
Camera

 Time needed:
10 minutes

Record video on your iPad

You probably didn't buy your iPad to record video, but it's an ability that shouldn't be overlooked

The old truism that the best camera is the one you have with you applies as much to shooting video as it does to taking snapshots. You might be browsing the internet, reading a book or listening to music on your iPad, but within seconds you can use it to quickly grab priceless footage of that never-to-be-repeated moment.

In fact, the iPad 2 and new iPad are equipped with two cameras: one front and one rear-facing. And while you'll probably get a lot of use out of the front-facing camera thanks to the FaceTime and Photo Booth apps, the better quality of the rear camera makes it more suitable for recording video.

While you can't really argue that the iPad allows the sort of unobtrusive video recording of its much smaller iPod touch or iPhone siblings – to be fair, using it to shoot video does feel a bit awkward the first time you do it – the tablet device's large screen makes it surprisingly easy to produce good results, particularly when it comes to focusing and exposure settings.

Once you've taken the footage, it's also simple to process and edit the results to send to friends or family. Here's how to get the best out of it.

Camera Shooting video with the iPad

01 Launch the video
Tap the Camera app's icon on your iPad's screen to launch it. Slide the Camera/Video slider (bottom right) toward the video camera icon to turn the video camera on.

02 Record video
Tap the record button to begin recording. As you record, the red record button will slowly pulse, while at the top right of the screen the elapsed time is displayed.

03 Change focus or exposure
To change the focus of the video or set its exposure tap at the point where you want to set the focus or the exposure, and the rest of the video will adjust to compensate.

Recording video footage
How to control your camera

Front or back?
When you're not recording, an icon appears in the upper-right corner of the screen that lets you switch between the front and rear cameras

Camera quality
You'll get better results with the rear-facing camera, which records HD video at up to 30 frames per second, than the lower-resolution front camera

Controlling recordings
The record button pulses as you record and the viewfinder displays the elapsed recording time. Just tap the Record button to stop recording

Lock focus
You can lock the focus and exposure by simply tapping and holding in the viewfinder until the focus box pulses and shows 'AE Lock'

Get the light right
The secret to capturing good quality video on the iPad is to make sure you use it in well-lit conditions. Both front and rear-facing cameras perform less well in low light conditions, so you'll get the best results if you record your video outside in the daytime or, if inside, where there is plenty of available light.

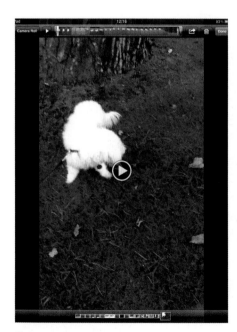

04 Stop recording
Tap the record button again to turn recording off. A thumbnail link to your freshly created video appears at the bottom left of the screen. Tap it to view the video you've just taken.

05 Edit the video
You can trim this video by dragging the start and end points on the filmstrip at the top of the screen and dragging the yellow handles inwards. When you're happy, tap the Trim button.

06 Share with others
To share your completed video with others, tap the arrow icon to the top right of the screen and select the appropriate option from the drop-down menu that appears.

The next step

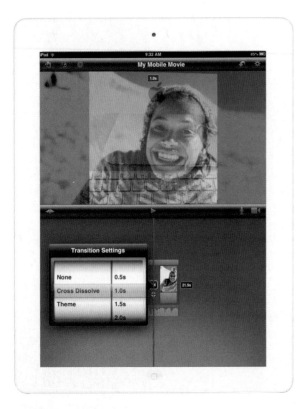

Edit a movie in iMovie

You can edit iMovie content as many times as you like and the results will always look professional

Touch is the key word when it comes to editing projects in iMovie on your iPad. You can swipe a clip up to the top of the screen to delete it, pull a bar to lengthen it or hold it to choose more subtle options. It can take a little bit of time to understand, but Apple has done an exceptional job of ensuring that, once learned, the system works as naturally as possible.

It is likely that every movie project will require some tweaking, so make sure you take some time to view what you have put together before converting it to a movie. It can take a while for the conversion process to complete – so be patient and be sure that your project looks right first time. If you want to create professional-looking movies with minimal editing, the app's trailer functionality is worth checking out because it ensures that your clips will flow and offers you lots of hints along the way.

This tutorial will give you the basics to get started, but remember the trick to creating professional content is to remove the need for editing as much as possible. However, iMovie lets you edit every part of every movie and the process is as natural as can be.

> "Apple has done an exceptional job of ensuring that, once learned, the system works as naturally as possible"

iMovie Edit iMovie projects

01 Tap to edit

All of the projects you have created in iMovie will be shown on the front screen. Simply tap one to open the project to start the editing process. The resulting screen will look familiar.

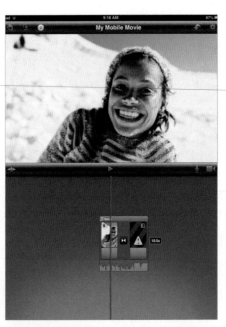

02 Delete clips

If you need to delete specific clips in a project after you have viewed the movie, simply hold it with your finger and swipe it up the screen. It will disappear immediately from the project.

03 Move clips

To move clips within the project you need to hold your finger down on one and then move it to the desired place within the timeline. You will use this technique often as you get more experienced.

All the tools you need

Multiple utilities in one screen

Clip timings
You can adjust the length of each individual clip by moving the yellow bars left and right. Tapping each clip will make them available and they are easy to manage

Total changes
With this icon you can change the entire theme of your movie as well as the start and end transitions. Try each one to see which works the best for the content you have included

Detailed information
Information is shown on screen as you make adjustments so that you can be sure that everything will flow as you want it to. It's the perfect balance between simplicity and complexity

Clever transitions
Tapping the icons between each clip lets you change the transitions to fade in and fade out as you prefer. You can choose different transitions for each clip to add variety

Movies and projects
As you edit projects you need to be aware that this will not change the movies you have already exported. They are saved files which will stay the same until you delete them. Each edited project needs to be converted again to create a new movie.

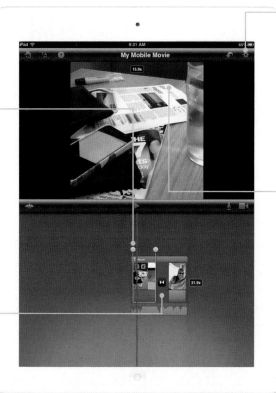

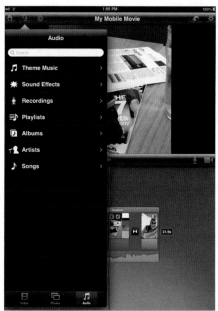

04 Project settings
Video clips that are used within a project will need to be managed. Hit the cog icon in the top-right to select an appropriate theme or choose to fade in or out from or to black.

05 Different trimming types
Be aware that when you trim a photo it just changes the amount of time it is displayed for, but video clip trimming will cut out some of the video that has been selected.

06 Sync the audio
Pay special attention to the audio track length and try to change the length of your clips accordingly. Ideally you will want the visuals and images or videos to finish at the same time.

The next step

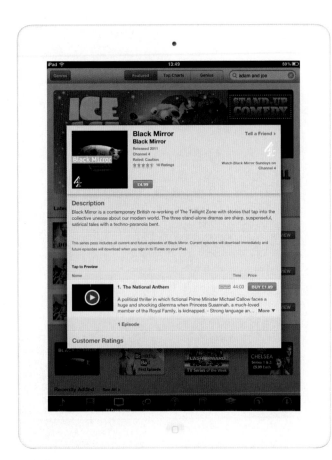

App used: Videos
Time needed: 10 minutes

Get the most out of iPad videos

The iPad is perfectly designed for the mobile movie experience thanks to its large screen

The Videos feature alone has the potential to keep you occupied on long plane journeys, in hotels or waiting rooms, and adds a use to the iPad that could justify half of the cost straight away. It has been designed for ease of use, as most Apple software is, and takes care of many of the niggles found in competing devices. For example, it will automatically play a film from the point you left it, and expanding the screen requires a simple double tap.

Everything is designed to help you get the most from the experience, but some tips are still useful to get you off to a flying start. In this step-by-step we will show you how to obtain new movies, how to transfer them to your iPad and how to make the most of the viewing experience. You could easily do all of this yourself, but in this instance a little knowledge certainly goes a long way and missing out on the movie capabilities of the iPad would be a real shame given the benefits it offers.

"The Video feature alone adds a use to the iPad that could justify half of the cost straight away"

Videos Make the most of movies

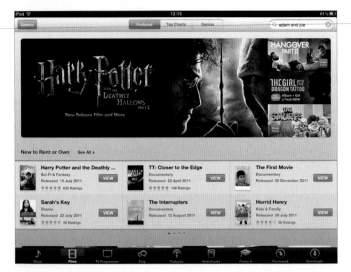

01 Grab a film

The easiest way to obtain good quality content is via iTunes. Navigate to the Films or TV Programmes section and choose the film you would like to rent or buy. You can also try some free trailers to get started without spending any money.

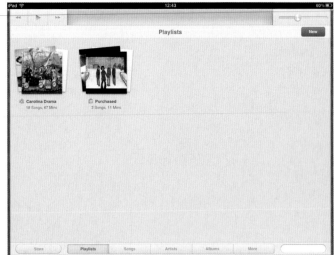

02 Put it on the iPad

Your purchases will be downloaded and stored on your iPad. If you have iCloud activated then they will also automatically be pushed to your other devices, such as your Mac or iPhone wirelessly, allowing you to view them on those devices too.

Watch movies on your iPad

Get the most out of the Videos app

Full screen
Tapping on this icon will alternate between full-screen and widescreen viewing. You can also double tap anywhere on screen to achieve this effect

Full control
You can move to specific parts of a video by moving the slider at the top with your finger; the further down the screen your finger is, the more precise the movement

Back where you left off
Videos automatically remembers where you finished watching and will start any film at that exact place when you open it up again

Main controls
The main control keys are standard and are brought up by tapping the screen once. You can play, pause, forward or rewind when you need to

HD
Many iTunes movies and TV programmes are now offered in HD format, which offers a much crisper viewing experience. Sometimes you will pay more for the video, but think of it in a similar way to paying more for Blu-ray. These files will also be larger in size, sometimes significantly, so make sure you have adequate space before you buy.

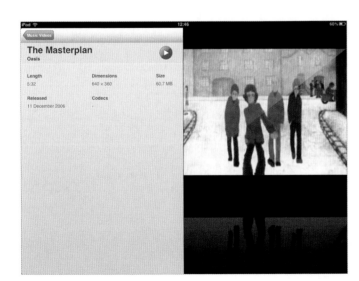

03 The fun starts here

All you need to do now is simply click the Videos icon and choose the film you want to watch from the list of videos that you have installed on your iPad. The film (or TV programme, for that matter) will immediately start to play from the beginning.

04 Small changes

Double-tapping the screen will make the movie play in full-screen mode, and doing so again will take it back to standard format (which is useful for widescreen films). The rest of the on-screen tweaks are obvious in their implementation, such as play, pause, etc.

App used:
YouTube

 Time needed:
10 minutes

Access video content via YouTube

Discover how to get the most out of YouTube on your iPad

 The built-in YouTube iPad app is a lesson in thoughtful design, and manages to bring the desktop experience to a mobile device while maintaining all of the functionality of the main web portal YouTube uses. With a YouTube account in place you can save favourites, share videos with friends and comment on videos you like, and your changes will be accessible on your desktop automatically. It all sounds very simple and on the whole it is, but some pointers will help you to get even more out of the experience.

It is worth remembering that, should you use the service on a 3G iPad, you will be pushing a hefty amount of data so be aware of the limits your network provider has imposed on your account. Wi-Fi is the recommended solution for YouTube-use on an iPad because it speeds up the loading of videos and also makes the experience feel more like the one you have come to expect on a desktop. The iPad YouTube app really does bring every feature to your mobile life, and here we will show you how to get up and running in no time and how to make the most of its potential. It's all free so you have no reason not to try it for yourself.

YouTube   Make the most of YouTube

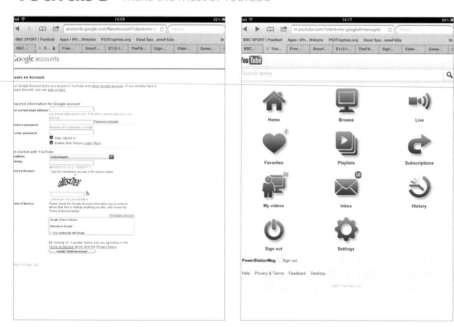

01 Get started

To utilise every feature in YouTube for the iPad you will need an account. Go to **www.youtube. com** and click the Create Account option in the top right-hand corner.

02 Create an account

Complete the requested information and then set up a new Google account (or use your current account in the next page). This completes the process for setting up a new YouTube account.

03 Make YouTube personal

On the iPad, open the YouTube app and tap Favourites, then tap the Sign In icon, and input your username and password. You will now have access to your videos, favourites and more.

YouTube on iPad

Once you discover how to use YouTube on your iPad, you may decide to use it as a replacement for the desktop version

Popular videos
The most recent popular videos of all time, from the past week and from today are a useful way to simply browse and see what's happening on YouTube

Keep it personal
Your main account information is kept up to date and is easily accessible via the handy icons at the bottom of each section

Search everything
You can search almost the entire YouTube database from your iPad in the same way you use a standard web search engine by typing in this box

Previews
Each video is previewed with an icon, rating and the number of views, which together should tell you if it's worth watching

Streaming
Streaming video wirelessly is very bandwidth-hungry, and overuse on 3G alone could cause you to break the limit on your data account. Your network provider is then within its rights to send you a warning. When possible, try to use Wi-Fi because this will not only perform better, but could potentially save you a lot of money.

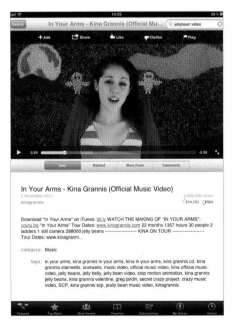

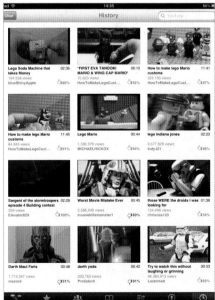

04 Explore the content
You can now explore the content within YouTube. When you tap a video to watch it you will see a selection of icons at the top of the screen that you can use to mark favourites or share videos.

05 Fully in step
Any changes that you make to your YouTube account on the iPad will be mirrored on your desktop, and vice versa, so you can use both and keep the changes intact.

06 Keep track
YouTube includes a history icon (found along the bottom of the screen) that shows your most recently viewed videos. This is useful if you forget to add a viewed video to your favourites list.

 App used:
Game Center

 Time needed:
10 minutes

Set up a Game Center account

Enter into a world of fun games, fierce competition and social gaming with Game Center

 Like Open Feint before it, Apple's Game Center is a multi-purpose gaming service that gives users a platform to befriend other gamers, engage in multiplayer, compete for online leaderboard supremacy and earn unlockable achievements. It comes preloaded on devices with iOS 4 and above installed, and it significantly enhances your iPad as a gaming platform.

Once you follow the initial set-up instructions, there is a wealth of options available to you. From the top menu you can clearly see your friend, game and achievement counters displayed, while the bottom tab bar lets you access Game Center's menus. 'Games' is by far the most in-depth, displaying all of your Game Center-enabled games, as well as your global ranking on the online leaderboards, something many people can become obsessed with.

Within each game's menu, you can also see how many achievements you have unlocked, get details on locked achievements and recommend the app to a friend. It's a solid service that brings together the best games available on one dedicated platform.

"It significantly enhances your iPad as a gaming platform"

Game Center Set up your new account

01 Get updated

Game Center runs on iPads running iOS 4 and above. It's unlikely your device will be running anything less, but it always pays to ensure your iPad is running the latest firmware available. Hook it up to iTunes and download any new updates before proceeding.

02 Open an account

Once in Game Center, tap the 'Create New Account' option. The app will ask you to input your location and date of birth, as well as accepting the terms and conditions. This is straightforward, but the next step requires a bit of thought.

Welcome to Game Center
Enter a world of fun and friends

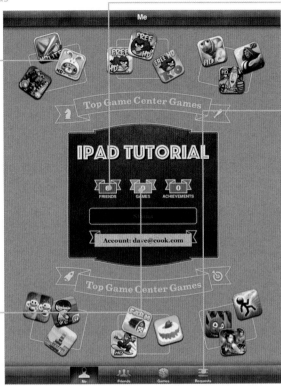

Your Friends list
Tapping 'Friends' will bring up a list of your connected friends, together with their achievements and recent games. In order for them to appear here, you must accept their friend request

Requests list
The 'Requests' tab houses your pending friends requests. You can also send out requests if you know the email address tethered to a person's Apple ID. Once a request is accepted, the person is instantly added to your list

Top Game Center games
Promoted or top-selling apps will refresh along the top and bottom of Game Center's top menu. You can tap app icons to be taken to their respective iTunes pages to buy them

The Games tab
Tapping 'Games' will bring up an overview of all your Games Center-enabled apps. Here, you can view achievements, online leaderboard rank, and recommend the app to friends

Rival platforms
Just like the console gaming world, iTunes plays host to two competing game platforms – Open Feint and Game Center – both vying for a place as the best gaming format the iOS has to offer. Both services have a wealth of superb features, such as Game Center's social features and Open Feint's free game deals. Both are well worth trying.

03 Register with iTunes
On the next page, you will be asked to input more data. Entering the email address associated with your existing Apple ID will automatically add your Game Center-enabled apps to the library. Otherwise, enter an unassociated email address to start from scratch.

04 Start playing today
Once your details have been entered, the app will return to the top menu. In the 'Games' tab you can get your account started properly by tapping 'Find Game Center Games'. This will take you straight to iTunes so you can start building your library.

The next step

Get to know the Music app

We guide you around your iPad's Music app and show you how to make a playlist

Your iPad's Music app is your mobile music player and superstore all rolled into one. With a clean, simple, easy-to-manipulate interface that is great fun to play with, you can play any tracks stored in your library by tapping on it and using the payback controls; create your own Playlists on the fly; and even visit the iTunes Store from within the app to buy something new. What's more, if you have enabled your iCloud (the free cloud storage and syncing service that comes free with iOS 5 and above), any new music you purchase will be pushed to all of your iOS devices without you having to lift a finger. By the same process you can also access and download music that you have downloaded in the past at no extra cost.

In this tutorial we guide you through the intricacies of this versatile app and show you how to create Playlists, access your purchased music files and much more.

Music Create a playlist

Launch the app
The previously named iPod app was updated in iOS 5 and is now known as the Music app. This can be found in your Dock by default. To get started, click on its icon and launch the app.

Browse songs
Use the tiles at the bottom of the screen to browse your music by Playlist, Songs, Artists or Albums. Tap on a song to start playing it. The playback controls are at the top of the screen.

Make a Playlist
Tap on the Playlist tile and then tap 'New' in the top-right corner. Give your new Playlist a name, then add songs from your library, drag them into a preferred order and then tap 'Done'.

Music while you're mobile

Setting up playlists on the iPad is a breeze

Playback controls

The playback controls, including play/pause, fast forward and rewind, are situated across the top of the Music app window, along with the volume slider and details about the song that is currently playing

Full control

You can move to specific parts of a video by moving the slider at the top with your finger; the further down the screen your finger is, the more precise the movement

Library tabs

The tiles at the bottom of the screen let you browse your music library in whatever way you wish. There is also a handy search window to the right

More music

You can purchase and download additional music at any time by tapping on the 'Store' button. This will take you to what is essentially the iTunes app, but it saves a little time

iTunes in the Cloud

You can still add converted CD tracks on your Mac to your iPad by connecting then two and dragging them across, but with iCloud enabled you can get any new purchased music pushed to all of your devices, including your Mac and your iPhone.

Visit the iTunes Store

You can make new purchases from within the Music app by tapping the 'Store' button. You can then browse the full iTunes Store and download new tracks, albums and podcasts.

Connect to iCloud

Through iCloud you can get all of your previous iTunes purchases beamed directly to your iPad. Create an account and connect, then go to the 'Purchased' category in the iTunes Store.

Get familiar with the settings

Go to 'Settings' and then tap 'Music' to access the app's preferences. Here you can set the EQ to the style of music you are playing, set a cap on how high the volume goes and more.

App used:
iTunes

Time needed:
5 minutes

Create Genius playlists on the iPad

Making your own special playlist is great but by letting the iPad do all the hard work you can get some really cool musical mixes

Keeping track of all the music on your iPad can be a bit of a pain. It's surprising how much music you can fit onto even just the 16GB version. With all that music it makes sense to keep track of it all and to create playlists.

Of course, listening to whole albums is fine, but then we all have our favourite tracks and like to hear them more often than others. Creating playlists manually is a great way of doing this, but it's time consuming and if you don't keep them updated they soon get rather tiresome.

You could just stick your whole music collection on random, but even this throws up issues like those hidden tracks or fillers that ruin a smooth transition, or the odd song you're bored of hearing. The best solution may well be Genius mixes.

Apple has created a tool that lets you select a track and automatically create a playlist of music that complements each other. It's a great way of keeping the music going around a certain theme and in the main it's incredibly reliable.

"We all have our favourite tracks and like to hear them more often than others"

Music Make Genius mixes on the iPad

01 Open Music

Fire up your iPad and then launch the new-look Music application. Your music can be displayed in a number of ways using the tabs along the bottom. Scroll until you find a song that would make a good foundation for your playlist; this will be the basis of your list.

02 Make a Genius mix

When you have found a track that most suits your current mood, tap on it to start it playing. When you're ready, tap on the Genius symbol that you can find across the top bar next to the running time and the name, artist and album name.

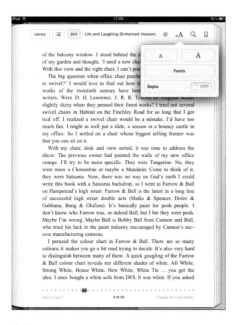

04 Font it

Tap on the 'aA' font button at the top to access the menu where you can alter the book's font and text size. Tap the big A to increase font size and the small one to decrease it.

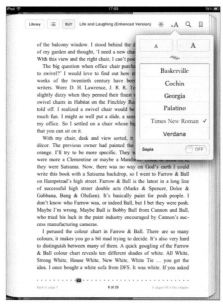

05 Font type

To change the font type, tap the Fonts button and then pick from the available options that are listed in the pop-out window. The selection should provide an alternative that suits you.

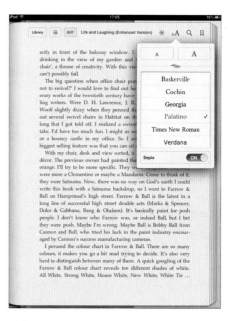

06 Tick it, watch it

Tap the font you wish to select and a tick will appear next to it. As with all the other changes you can make to the appearance of a book within iBooks, they happen instantly.

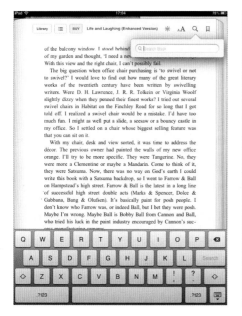

07 Spotlight index

Tap on the magnifying glass icon to bring up a search field. Every book on the iBook Store is fully indexed so you can instantly find individual words in a book – invaluable for textbooks.

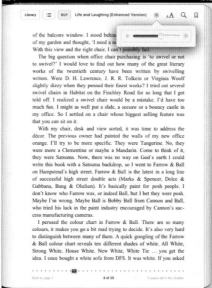

08 Brightness

Tap on the sunshine icon to bring up brightness settings of the book. This only affects the levels within iBooks and doesn't translate to the rest of the iPad, so you won't have to change it back.

09 Suitable setting

Changing the brightness means that you can alter the reading light to whatever is most comfortable for your eyes. The brighter the ambient light, the brighter iBooks needs to be.

The next step

Set up a subscription on Newsstand

The built-in app allows you to subscribe to your favourite magazines and get the new issue on release day

One of the great new features of iOS 5 was the Newsstand app, which lets you keep on top of all your favourite reading with ease. This built-in app enables you to create your own personal magazine library, and has its own dedicated store for you to purchase and download from. The excitement for Newsstand stems from the fact that it means new developers have started afresh on their tablet publications, learning from previous mistakes to provide a better reading experience this time around for iOS 5 and later users. The other big positive with Newsstand is that you can set up subscriptions to your favourite magazines, so you never miss an issue, and have each one download to your Newsstand library and be accessible to you anywhere.

More and more magazines are becoming available via Newsstand and the App Store, so the amount of choice is growing constantly, each publication trying to stand out from the crowd with interactive features and extra content. Setting up a subscription is a simple process and a good way to get your bearings should you be new to iOS.

"This built-in app enables you to create your own personal magazine library"

Newsstand Purchase a subscription

01 Open Newsstand
On your Home screen, tap the Newsstand icon to open up the app and see your current library of magazine titles on the shelves. This is where all your downloaded items are displayed.

02 Visit the Store
To start your magazine search, tap the Store button at the top right of the Newsstand display. This will take you to the dedicated Newsstand wing of the App Store.

03 Search the Store
Here you can browse through all the magazines on sale – either using the various breakdowns provided by the Store, or by tapping Featured or Release Date and then using the search bar.

Making sense of the Newsstand Store

Find your way around this magazine archive

Search
If you click Featured or Release Date, it will bring up a search box so you can do a more direct search of the App Store

Info
When you find a magazine for you, don't just tap Install; instead tap the icon and get the extra info, including reviews and cost of each issue

Featured titles
At the top of this page is the animated Featured window, where a selection of the most popular titles are displayed and so this is a good place to start your browsing

Menu tabs
Along the bottom of the screen you have various tabs to help you navigate, including charts of the bestselling apps as well as Genius, which offers you download suggestions

Auto Subscriptions
Always keep track of your subscriptions as some automatically renew without you physically tapping to do so. Make a note if a title you download tells you this, which it will do, so you don't get a nasty surprise when you get your bank statement six months after you thought a subscription had ended.

04 Install and download
Once you've found the title you were after, tap Install and enter your iTunes password to download it to your Newsstand library, where you can access back issues and set up subscriptions.

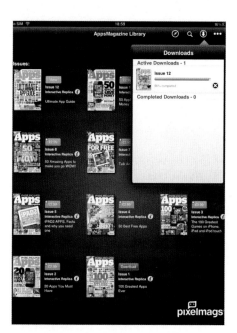

05 What's on offer
It may take a few minutes for the title to download, but once it has, tap the cover to enter its personal library, and tap the Subscribe icon to see what options are on offer before purchasing.

06 Start reading
Once you've chosen your subscription and entered your password, the latest issue will become available in the magazine's library. Tap it to download, and start reading.

App used:
Pages

Time needed:
10 minutes

Get to grips with Pages

Apple's Pages takes the mobile word-processing experience to a whole new level

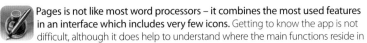

Pages is not like most word processors – it combines the most used features in an interface which includes very few icons. Getting to know the app is not difficult, although it does help to understand where the main functions reside in order to get you started, and doing so will open up the power within. Despite the rather sparse interface, it is packed with formatting options and clever little tricks that make previously tiresome manoeuvres a thing of the past. For example, you can move an embedded image around an article and the words will automatically reposition themselves around it, and the included templates are completely customisable, which enables you to get creating in no time at all.

Not all specific needs are catered for, such as a word count, but Apple has done a good job of defining the most used functions that people need and being able to share your creations without touching a desktop is another advantage. You can even decide which format to save these documents in and, best of all, if you have iCloud enabled then you can sync your pages wirelessly between devices – so you can start a new layout on your iPad and finish it later on your iPhone or Mac. In this tutorial we guide you through the basics of this incredible versatile app.

Pages Create stunning documents on the move

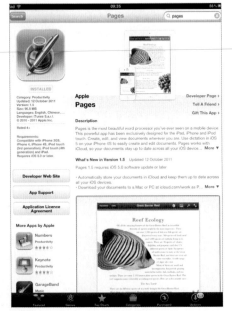

01 Grab the app
Search for 'Pages' in iTunes and purchase and install as normal. £6.99/$9.99 may seem expensive for an iTunes app, but it is in fact very good value for a word processor with so many features.

02 Have a look around
Pages is so obviously visual in the way it is designed that you could just have a wander around the icons and start typing, but the best place to start is the pre-loaded user manual.

03 Create your first document
In the first screen tap the '+' icon at the top and then tap New document. This will bring up a screen with templates on. You can choose anything from a blank page to a party invitation.

Making the most of Pages

Learn all the tricks of the Pages trade

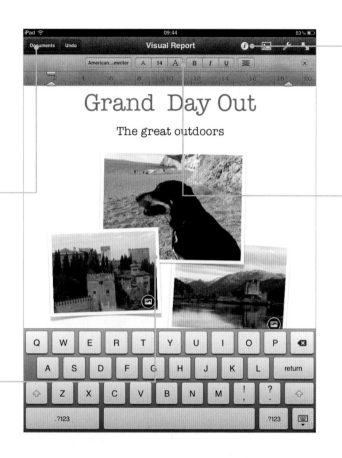

Document handling
Your completed documents are never far away. A tap of the 'My Documents' icon will bring up a page showing all of your saved work. Each document is saved automatically after every change

Extra formatting
Simply tap the 'i' icon to access extra formatting features such as bullet points, subtitles and headings. The options automatically change if you have an image highlighted

All the standards
All of the standard formatting options such as bold, italics and underline are easily accessible from the top bar. Highlight a word and click an icon for the desired effect

Work with templates
Templates can make the process of creating eye-catching documents incredibly easy and Pages includes a variety of styles. Once you create a new document using a template you can change the images and all of the background text to your needs. You can also create your own templates for future use.

Easy image manipulation
Once inserted, images can be resized, moved and even twisted to the position you need. The words will automatically move to around them and into the right position

04 Test the options
Type a few words and then check the formatting options at the top. Select words by tapping and holding, at which point you can use the icons to format the text. Clicking 'i' gives further options.

05 Delve deeper
Other options include a document setup wizard, defined by the top-right spanner icon and a quick tap of the picture icon lets you insert an image into your document.

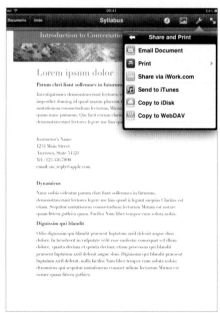

06 Share your work
You never need to save your work because Pages does it whenever a change is made, but you can export it to PDF, Pages or Word format and send by email with the tap of one icon.

The next step

Create spreadsheets with Numbers

Use Numbers to create serious or silly spreadsheets to suit all tastes

App used: Numbers **Time needed:** 10 minutes

Spreadsheets are a part of everyone's lives these days and have taken on multiple roles in business and at home. Most spreadsheet programs tend to focus on the business side because this is where they are mainly used, but spreadsheets have a myriad of other uses that aren't often explored.

Numbers puts multiple uses front and centre with special templates built in and also brings a new way of working to the mobile user. However, the interface and function locations may feel alien to those that have used Excel for a long time and so a short introduction will help you to get to grips with the app quickly. There are a lot of functions built in to Numbers and some of these are not obvious, so take a look at these simple steps to start number-crunching straight away.

Tabs, tabs, tabs
You can create as many linked tabs as you like by simply tapping the '+' icon. When you need to view them, just move your finger from left to right until you find the one that you need

Touchy feely
You can adjust and select single cells, rows and columns with your finger and even though it feels strange at first, you will soon wonder how you ever created spreadsheets with just a mouse

Four icons
These four small icons are the shop window to a huge array of advanced functions including specialised calculations and standard formats

"Mainly used in business, spreadsheets have many other uses that aren't often explored"

Numbers Explore the power of this spreadsheet app

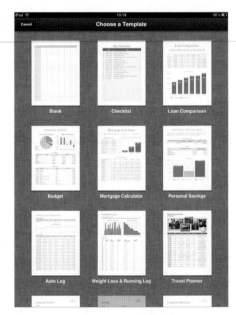

01 Grab the app
Numbers is available from the App Store. It costs £6.99/$9.99, and although this may seem steep, it is excellent value even if you only need spreadsheets occasionally.

02 Check out the manual
Apple has included a manual in Numbers which highlights the various solutions it can be used for. Because of the large number of features on offer, it is recommended that you read it all.

03 Your first spreadsheet
Tap the '+' icon at the top and click the New Spreadsheet option. You'll now be offered a choice of templates which includes everything from a blank sheet to a mortgage calculator.

134 iPad for Beginners

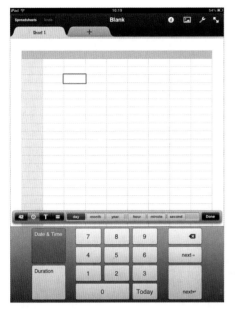

04 Add data

Choose the blank template option in the top-left corner and double-tap an empty cell. This brings up a dialog with four icons for numbers, date/time, text and formulas.

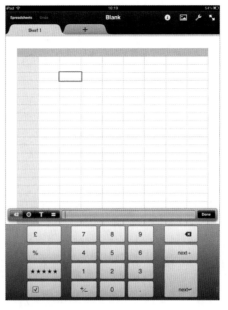

05 Handy shortcuts

Tapping any of the icons brings up a dialog with shortcuts pertinent to the data you want to input. For example the number icon will bring up a number pad plus a percentage button and more.

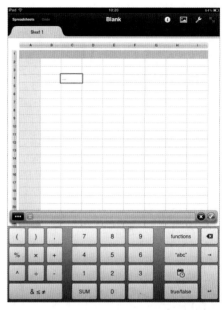

06 Use the data

Once you've understood where each function resides you can now do something with your content. Tap the '=' icon and you can choose from a wide range of simple functions that will pop up.

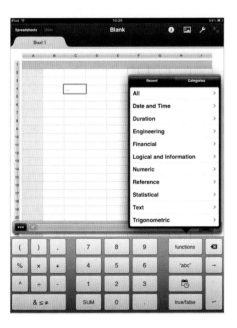

07 Advanced functions

The functions button is a window to some serious capability and includes categories of advanced functions such as Trigonometric, Engineering and Statistical.

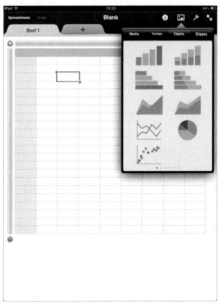

08 Add some media

Once you have your basic data built you can tap the picture icon in the top-right and insert photos, tables and shapes which will help to make the data more visual.

09 Practise your touch

Numbers is touch only and this will present problems at first, but the more you practise the more natural it begins to feel. The interface looks simple, but it hides a huge range of options.

The next step

 App used: Keynote
 Time needed: 10 minutes

Perform your presentations in style with Keynote

Keynote for iPad brings the Apple ethos of keeping things simple to the world of presentations

CHESS – A Whole New 'Take'

The classic hit musical gets re-imagined for 2012. If you think that you *know it so well*, prepare to be blown away! Oh Yeah!

Creating presentations in PowerPoint has caused as much scratching of heads over the years as almost any other software solution. Despite this, it has been widely used in the corporate world and still dominates the presentation software market. Keynote for iPad brings the advantages of being mobile and incredibly easy to use.

Because the iPad is finger driven, Apple has had to do away with the preciseness this type of software normally requires and has managed to make the entire process finger-friendly and much quicker than the competition. It will still take some time to get used to, though, because the commands are different and at times it feels almost too easy. In this guide we will show you how to create your first presentation and how to make the most of the features and the fact that you can create wherever you are without the need for wires.

"Apple has managed to make the entire presentation process finger-friendly and much quicker"

Using Keynote

Make your presentations look professional without needing to touch your desktop PC or Mac

Use the icons
These four simple icons hold within them a wealth of tweaks and tricks that will help you build a presentation in no time at all

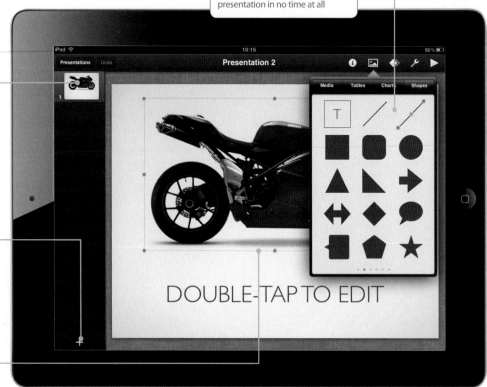

Check your slides
All of your slides are available in the left-hand column and are previewed in great detail. You can also drag and drop them to change the order in which they will appear

New slides
Adding a new slide requires a single tap on the '+' icon. Almost every function in Keynote only requires a tap or two and is highly intuitive to use

Shapes, text and more
The media available is almost unlimited and everything from simple text to photos and charts are available to you. You can then manipulate them once inserted into a slide

DOUBLE-TAP TO EDIT

136 iPad for Beginners

Keynote Build a Keynote presentation

01 Get Keynote
Keynote is available on the iTunes App Store for £6.99/$9.99 and is part of the iWork for iPad solution. All you need to do is purchase it and install it on your iPad as normal.

02 Read the manual
As you would expect from Apple, a comprehensive manual is included in the app which is effectively designed to get you up and running quickly.

03 Create your first presentation
Click the '+' icon at the bottom and then select New Presentation. You can choose from 12 themes, but for the purposes of this guide select the White one.

04 Build your first slide
On the first slide, double-tap the photo and tap the small icon that pops up. You can replace the photo with an image of your choice from the photo library.

05 Use your words
Double-tap the text and add your own words. When done, tap on the words and tap the 'i' icon. This will bring up a selection of styles and colours for the text.

06 The important second slide
Tap the '+' icon on the bottom-left to create a second slide. Tap the picture icon at the top and then choose the 'Shapes' tab. Tap the 'T' to insert a new text box.

07 Add media
You will have noticed from the previous step that you are able to insert photographs, tables, charts and a variety of different shapes through the one command.

08 Time for tweaks
You can manipulate your media easily within Keynote. Tap a photograph and then hold two fingers on it – you can now spin it round to any angle you like.

09 Share your work
Once you have finished, you are able to share your work by tapping the left icon in the main document view. This will let you send it via email or to iWork.com.

App used:
AirPlay

 Time needed:
10 minutes

Stream content with AirPlay

You can turn your iPad into your home media hub that all the family can share by streaming audio and video to other devices in your house. Here's how

While it's great to be able to carry your favourite films, photos and music with you on your iPad, let's be honest: the joy is a personal one, as the iPad's speakers and screen are hardly built for sharing with a wider audience.

Or at least it would be without the iPad's killer feature: AirPlay. It allows you to stream your iPad's music, video and images wirelessly across a local network.

The only extra you need to use AirPlay is a compatible device to stream your iPad's content to. This could be an AppleTV, AirPlay-enabled stereo speakers – of which there are several on the market – or an AirPort Express wireless base station, which comes with a socket that enables it to connect to a home stereo system. A button tap is all it takes to free your audio and video and watch films on the big screen, or listen to your music collection on your best speakers. No wires required.

"A tap is all it takes to free your audio and video and watch films on a big screen"

AirPlay · Set up your AirPlay connection

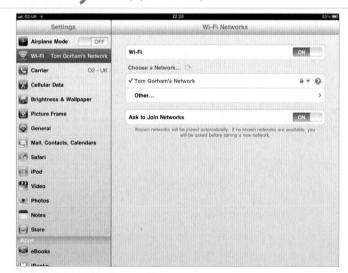

01 Check wireless settings

AirPlay works over a local Wi-Fi network, so check that your iPad and the device you're streaming to are on the same network. You can set this up on the iPad by tapping Settings and choosing the Wi-Fi option. If your network is secured, you will need to enter its password.

02 Open the media

When your devices are properly connected, start playing the media on the iPad that you want to stream to another device. When you play a movie or a song on your iPad tap the AirPlay icon (a hollow rectangle with a solid triangle) that appears on the media controller.

AirPlay on the iPad in action

AirPlay is an impressive technology, but
it's pretty simple to use

More than video
It is not just the media itself that can be sent over AirPlay. Song titles, artists, album names and even media artwork can all appear on AirPlay-enabled speakers that have graphical displays

Audio or video?
The speaker icon here indicates that only audio will be streamed to the external device. If you see a TV icon instead, video will also be streamed over AirPlay

AirPlay's icon
The AirPlay icon itself is just a simple box with an arrow. The same icon appears on all iOS devices, and in iTunes on the Mac and PC too

AirPlay everywhere
AirPlay is a clever wireless technology the usefulness of which isn't restricted to the iPad. In fact, any iOS device with iOS 4.2 or later installed on it can use AirPlay – and so can the iTunes application on Mac OS X. AirPlay features are also present in Apple's free Remote iPad and iPhone app, which allows you to control an iTunes library from an iOS device. But not all video can be streamed using AirPlay. At the time of writing, video streaming from the iPad is limited to media that is streamed from Apple's own apps – other apps can only stream audio.

03 Choose your output
When you tap the AirPlay icon, a pop-up menu will appear, offering a choice of AirPlay-enabled devices. The currently selected output displays a tick next to it, and it should be your iPad. Tap the name of the device that you would like to stream to.

04 Stream in action
Unfortunately, you are not able to watch the same video in two places at the same time. Once you have selected another output device from the list, the video or audio is sent there within just a couple of seconds. The iPad's screen will then go blank!

App used:
N/A

Time needed:
5 minutes

View iPad content on your Apple TV

If your iPad's screen isn't large enough, don't worry. With the help of Apple TV, you can use the big screen instead

It's safe to say that video mirroring is one of the iPad 2 and third-generation iPad's best kept secrets. It's so called because when activated, it mirrors the display of your iPad on a TV screen with the help of Apple TV.

That can have a number of obvious benefits. If you're tired of huddling around your iPad's screen when you share a video with your friends, you'll appreciate the ability to relax and view the video on a larger screen. Games take on a new dimension on the big screen, and some are even optimised for mirroring, showing the controls on your iPad, while the TV displays the action.

There are some limitations with video mirroring, though. For a start, mirroring isn't possible with the original iPad (you can't use it on iPod touches either, nor on iPhones before the iPhone 4S) and the iPad's aspect ratio doesn't match that of most TVs, so you'll probably see a black bar on either side of the screen. Some applications can display at full HD resolution, however.

The only other real drawback to video mirroring on your iPad is that it isn't always obvious how to turn it on. But that's something that's easy to address, and this tutorial's here to show you how to do it.

AirPlay Turn on video mirroring

01 Set it up
The controls for video mirroring aren't found in the iPad's Settings. Instead, double-tap the Home button to bring up the iPad's multitasking bar, which shows your recently used apps.

02 Select your Apple TV
Swipe your finger to the right and you should see the AirPlay icon next to the iPod controls. Tap the icon and you should see any Apple TVs connected to your Wi-Fi network in the list.

03 Turn mirroring on
Tap 'Apple TV' in the list to select it and, underneath, slide the 'Mirroring' option to the 'On' position. In a second or two, the iPad's Home screen should be visible on your TV.

Setting up mirroring
Getting the best out of AirPlay

iPad rotation
The display on your TV screen mimics the rotation of your iPad, so you'll probably get better results by rotating your screen to landscape mode

Newer iPads only
AirPlay only works on the second-generation Apple TV and on the latest iPads. Older devices just won't work

Play your videos
To play an iPad video full-screen on your TV, tap the Videos app then tap the AirPlay icon

Using full screen
Some apps, such as Real Racing HD, will adjust their display to expand into full-screen on your TV

Mirroring with wires
Don't have an Apple TV or a wireless connection? Apple also sells an HDMI adapter cable that can link your iPad and TV directly through the latter's HDMI port. The results are as good as using AirPlay wirelessly, but of course, the cable will restrict your iPad's movements.

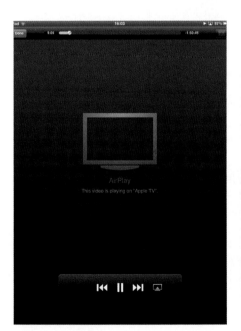

04 Run AirPlay
Now everything that appears on your iPad will also be displayed on the larger TV screen. As confirmation, the iPad's title bar turns blue and shows the Airplay icon.

05 Rotate the iPad
AirPlay will respect the aspect ratio of your iPad, so unless you're using a full-screen app, it won't fill the screen. But you can rotate the iPad and the rotation will change the display on the screen too.

06 Play streaming video
You can play streaming HTML video full screen by navigating to the video, then tapping the AirPlay icon that appears next to it. It will now expand to play on your TV screen.

App used:
AirPrint

Time needed:
10 minutes

Print from your iPad with AirPrint

Yes, believe it or not, you can actually print from your iPad – but there are some tricks you should know first. Here are our secrets to iPad printing

When critics sought to find flaws in the iPad on its release, one weakness they focused on was its inability to print. At the time, for a permanent record of anything on your iPad's screen you had to email a copy to your Mac or PC and print it from there.

But the arrival of iOS 4.2 ended those complaints by bringing printing to the iPad's set of features. And in true Apple fashion it's a cinch to use – even if it does have limitations.

AirPrint works with most popular iPad applications, such as Pages, Safari and Photos. It works over a local Wi-Fi network, so in order to use it you need to be on the same network as the printer that you plan to use. The catch is that the iPad only prints to AirPrint-compatible printers, currently restricted to a limited range (a full list can be found at http://bit.ly/euwjbk). But the good news is that some third-party utilities enable you to print to any printer on your network.

"AirPrint works with most popular iPad applications, such as Pages and Safari"

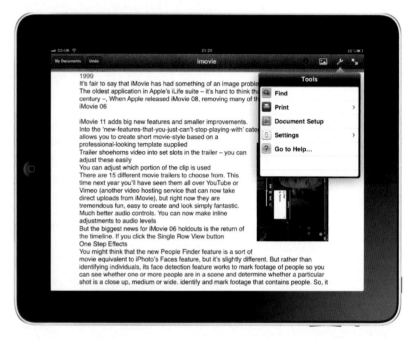

AirPrint How to print a webpage

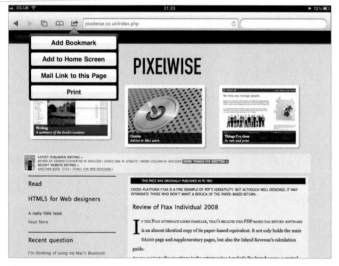

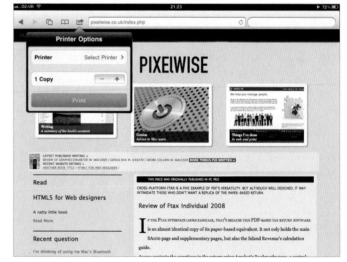

01 Choose the page to print

Many iPad apps now support printing, and most use the same technique. To print a page in Safari, for example, navigate to the page you want to print, click the arrow icon at the top of the screen, and select the Print option from the drop-down menu.

02 Choose the printer

Your iPad doesn't automatically know which printer you want to print to. The first time you print from an application, you will be prompted to select a printer. You will have to tap Select Printer to make your choice from the available printers.

Printing on the iPad

Most iPad apps follow the same approach when printing

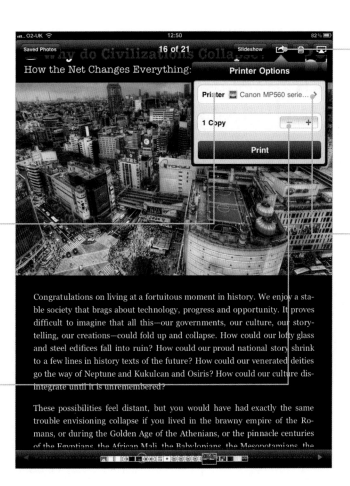

Find the Print icon
In most apps that support printing, the printing option is found under the same 'arrow in box' icon

Options
Currently Apple restricts the type of printer you can print to, but here we're using the Printopia utility to print to a non-AirPrint-compatible Canon printer

Switching printers
The iPad remembers your chosen printer, but if you want to change the one you would like to use, tap the printer in the list and you will be taken to another drop-down menu showing all available options

Number of copies
Quickly choose the number of copies you would like to print by tapping the '+' or '-' buttons. Depending on the options that your printer supports, you may see additional choices here

Print to any printer
So what do you do if you don't have an AirPrint-ready printer? One way around this limitation is to use Printopia (www.ecamm.com/mac/printopia), a Mac utility that when installed lets your iPad print to any printer attached to your Mac, even it isn't AirPrint compatible. It also adds a 'virtual printer' that lets you send PDFs or JPEGs directly from your iPad straight to your Mac.

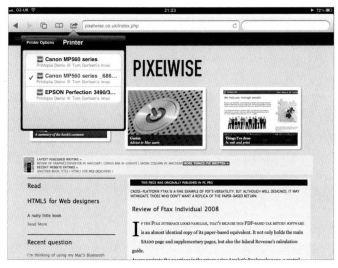

03 The printer list
As long as you are on the same Wi-Fi network as your printers, you should see every AirPrint-enabled device in this list. Simply choose the device that you would like to print the webpage to, so you can select any further printing options.

04 Choosing options
Depending on the printer you have selected. you may get other printing options. For example, if your printer supports double-sided printing, this may appear as an option. When you're happy with the options you have chosen, tap the 'Print' button and the page will be printed.

App used:
Twitter

Time needed:
10 minutes

Tweet from your iPad

Follow the day-to-day activities of your favourite folk and share the latest news from your own life with this super social networking app

As you'll probably know by now, Twitter enables you to share short messages (no more than 144 characters in length) with the rest of the world – much like the status updates in Facebook. Even if you don't have a Twitter account it's impossible to avoid the influence of this social networking site. Politicians, banks and your favourite TV personality are more likely to have a Twitter account than not, so that they can update you on their latest activities.

The iPad Twitter app enables you to subscribe to – or follow – the Twitter broadcasts of particular people. You can also broadcast – or tweet – your own thoughts, and you may pick up some followers along the way who will hang off your every word.

To follow this tutorial you'll need to install the free Twitter app from the iTunes Store. Once you launch the app you can click Sign Up to create your own Twitter account, or Sign In if you've already got one. We'll then show you how to make your own tweets and find interesting people to follow.

> "Even if you don't have a Twitter account you can't avoid the influence of this site"

Twitter Start tweeting with this app

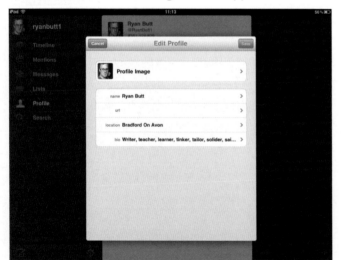

01 Set up a profile

To help future followers know who you are, click Profile, then Edit Profile. Click Profile Image to find a mug shot from your iPad's Photo Library – you'll need to use a small photo as Twitter doesn't like large files. Tap bio and write a brief description of yourself then click Save.

02 Make a tweet

To tweet, tap the icon at the screen's bottom left. Type into the New Tweet window. As you're limited to a message containing 144 characters, you'll see a countdown at the bottom left of the Tweet window. You can even attach a photo to the tweet. Click Send when you're ready.

Twitter in action

Get to know your way around the Twitter interface

Timeline

When any of the people that you follow make a tweet, it will appear in this scrolling Timeline page. To find out more about a particular person simply click on their photo and their profile page will then appear just to the right of the Timeline

Similar

This section provides an effective way of introducing you to new people to follow. If you're following a British comedian like Jimmy Carr, then you might enjoy keeping tabs on similar celebrities like Matt Lucas for example

Retweet

If you want to share someone's latest tweet with your own followers, click here and choose Retweet (or Quote Tweet) from the pop-up menu. This function enables particular news items or issues to get really amazing publicity

Make a tweet

Click here to open the New Tweet window. Tap out anything you want to share using the iPad's keyboard. Potential followers can find you if your tweet contains topics that they are searching for

Twitter iOS 6 integration

When you update to iOS 6, Twitter will become integrated into a host of Apple apps to make it more convenient to tweet than ever before. You will still need to download and install the free Twitter app, but once done, go to Settings and then tap on the 'Twitter' section. From here you can allow apps such as Photos, Safari, YouTube, Camera and Maps to use your Twitter account. Once set-up, you will then be able to tweet quickly and easily from within those apps without even having to leave them.

03 Follow that star

To find folk to follow, click Search and type in a name. Each person's Twitter ID is prefaced with an @ symbol. If you want to follow the head writer of *Doctor Who*, for instance, then click on @steven_moffat to see their Twitter profile. Their bio should confirm that you've got the right person. Click Follow.

04 Explore

Once you've found people to follow click on the Timeline icon. The latest tweets from the people you follow will appear. Tap on a person's photo to see their profile. You can then click their Tweets icon to see all their recent tweets. Swipe the screen to move between various open profiles.

App used: Twitter · Time needed: 5 minutes

Make use of Twitter integration

With Twitter integrated into iOS 6, instantly share thoughts, feelings and links from your favourite apps

There's little doubt that Twitter is a social phenomenon. This simple application allows you to share thoughts – or 'tweets' – with people around the world almost as soon as they enter your head, and likewise, see what's on the minds of people that you choose to follow.

The advent of smartphones has taken this concept to the next level by allowing you to tweet at any time, wherever you are in the world, making it easier than ever to speak your mind. In iOS 6, the tweeting process is easier than ever before.

Twitter is integrated seamlessly into Apple's latest operating system; simply sign in, then begin tweeting directly from your favourite apps. You no longer need to open a specific Twitter app, find a photo to upload or copy links from your web browser; simply do it directly from within the app. It's so easy that your Twitter activity will increase dramatically once you get to grips with it. In this tutorial, we guide you through setting up Twitter integration, and how to tweet from your favourite apps.

"Share your thoughts with the world and see what's on your friends' minds"

Twitter Tweet from within your favourite apps

01 Go to Settings
Choose Settings, then tap on the Twitter option in the left-hand column. If you don't already have Twitter installed, tap Install.

02 Log in
Enter your details – including your username and password – adjust the 'Find Me by Email' and Tweet Location options, and tap Done.

03 Tweet in Safari
Open Safari. To tweet about a page, tap the Add Bookmark option, and choose Tweet. A link to the page will be added to your tweet.

Integrating Twitter

Tweet easily from other apps

Camera comments
If your iPad has iOS 5 or iOS 6 installed on it, then you can also tweet from within the Camera app, allowing you to upload, comment and caption your pictures almost as soon as they are captured. Keeping others informed of your actions has never been so easy.

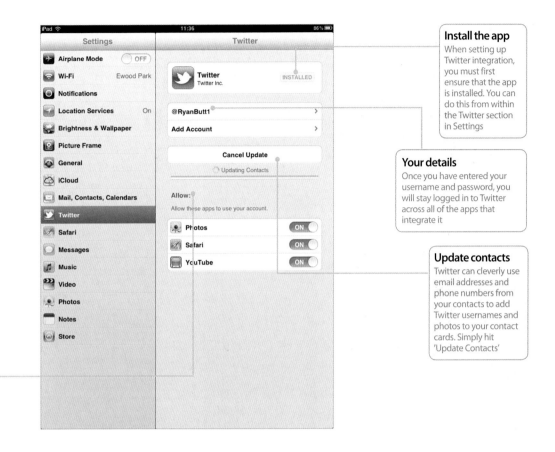

Install the app
When setting up Twitter integration, you must first ensure that the app is installed. You can do this from within the Twitter section in Settings

Your details
Once you have entered your username and password, you will stay logged in to Twitter across all of the apps that integrate it

Update contacts
Twitter can cleverly use email addresses and phone numbers from your contacts to add Twitter usernames and photos to your contact cards. Simply hit 'Update Contacts'

Grant permissions
In order to allow Twitter to become integrated with other apps, you must grant permission for particular apps to use your Twitter account

04 Tweet in Photos
When viewing an image, tap the share icon, and select Tweet. Any pictures you tweet about will be added as a link to your message.

05 Tweet in YouTube
Share videos in YouTube by tapping the Share button at the top of the viewing window, then Tweet. A link will be added to your message.

06 Tweet in Maps
Tweet your current location or places of interest by tapping on your current location, then the 'i' icon. Choose Share Location, then Tweet.

The next step

App used:
Facebook

Time needed:
5 minutes

Use Facebook in iOS 6

Discover why it's easier than ever to keep your friends and family in your social loop

With iOS 6, Apple has integrated Facebook as seamlessly as Twitter in iOS 5, so you can update your status without leaving your core apps. Interacting with the world's largest social network has never been easier. Now you can share a photo on Facebook straight from your Camera or Photos app, post your location using Maps, brag about high scores straight from Game Center and, if you have your hands full, you can get Siri to do all the posting on your behalf.

Just like with Apple's Twitter integration before it, you will need to download the free Facebook app and log in to your account to access the Facebook features on your iPad. But once you sign in, you'll be up and running and won't have to worry about logging in again. With the Facebook integration, you need never miss an important birthday or get-together again because all Facebook events are integrated straight into your Calendar app. With new iOS 6 Facebook integration, it has never been easier to keep your friends and family updated on the move.

"You can share a photo straight from your Camera or Photos app"

Facebook Let's have a look at the cool things you can do with Facebook in iOS 6 on your iPad

01 Get started

The first step will be to download the app from the App Store. Once you've done that, head to your iPad's Settings app and find Facebook's page. Sign in for your login details and enable the apps that you want Facebook to integrate with. Flick to 'On' position.

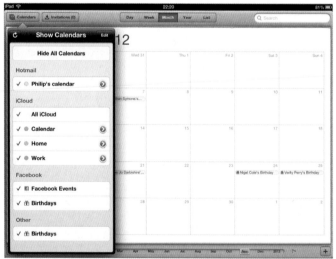

02 Import information

After letting Facebook sync with your Contacts app, you should now notice that your Calendar app has been updated with new 'Facebook Events' and 'Birthdays' information and all of your friends have been added to your Contacts app.

Setting up Facebook in iOS 6

How to ensure Facebook is seamlessly integrated into your everyday apps

Get the app
You will need to download and install the free Facebook app from the App Store to integrate it into the operating system. Once done, go to the Facebook section in Settings

Update All Contacts
When setting up the Facebook service for the first time, tap on this button and all of your Facebook friends' contact info will be imported into your Contacts app

Facebook Settings
Tap on this arrow in your Facebook Settings to configure your Chat and Message alerts and various other options that relate to the active Facebook account you are using

App integration
By enabling these options, your Contacts will be automatically updated whenever a Facebook friend changes their contact details. Facebook events and birthdays will also be added to your Calendar app

We 'Like' this
The Facebook 'Like' button is now part of iTunes and the App Store. So you can tell your Facebook friends that you Like songs, albums, shows, movies and apps without having to leave whatever app you are in. Now that's worth posting about!

03 Sharing photos
You can share photos to Facebook either from your iPad's Camera app or your Photos app. Just navigate to the picture you want to show off and tap the share button. In iOS 6 you'll find a new Facebook option. Choose Facebook to send the photo to your News Feed.

04 Facebook integration
Facebook has also been integrated into other core apps too, such as Maps (so you can share a location) and Game Center (so you can post scores and find new friends based on Facebook). You'll even find Facebook options in Safari now.

100 Essential Apps

Sort the wheat from the chaff with this comprehensive guide to the must-own apps for your iPad

The writer Theodore Sturgeon coined the adage '90 per cent of everything is crud'. As the Apple App Store has thousands of apps to choose from, it can be a daunting task to decide which ones to download, especially if you have to fork out your hard-earned cash.

This feature should help you fill your iPad with apps that are useful, informative and perhaps even life-saving! To help you find 'keepers' for your iPad, we'll give you an overview of the App Store's 20-plus categories and highlight five 'must-have' apps' from each one.

We'll unveil apps to keep you occupied and entertained, apps that turn reluctant cooks into credible chefs, apps that let non-musicians make sweet sounds, and apps to give you local knowledge even if you're in a strange neighbourhood. Having the right apps on your iPad can transform your life in many ways, so read on to discover which ones we recommend and why.

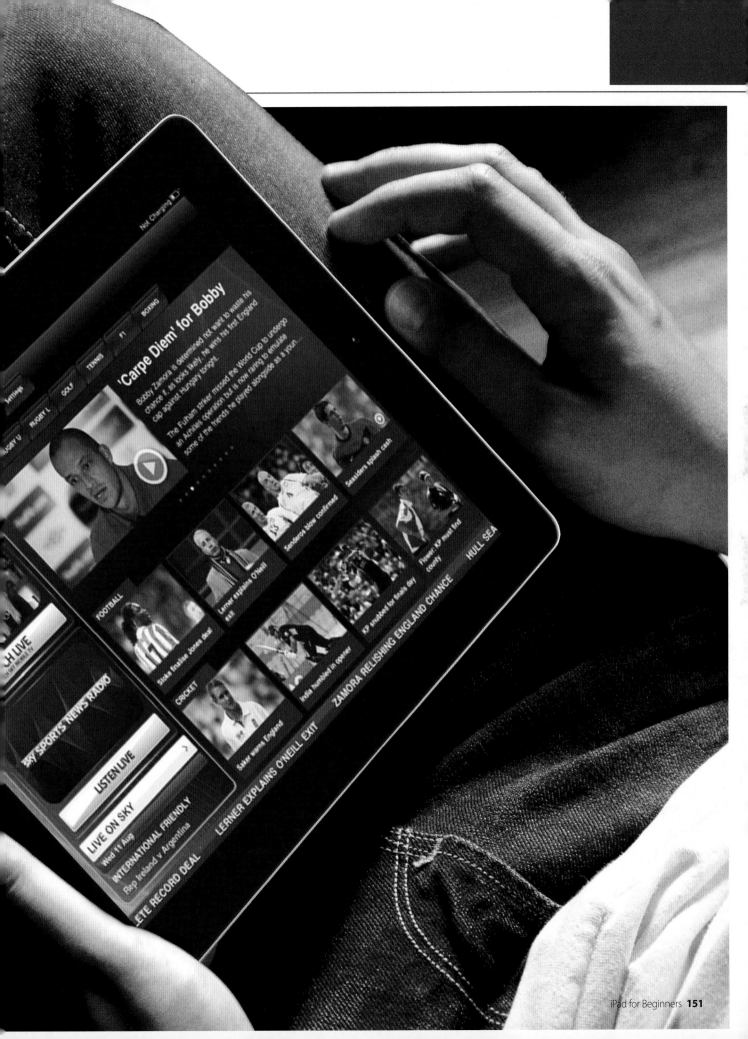

Essential apps

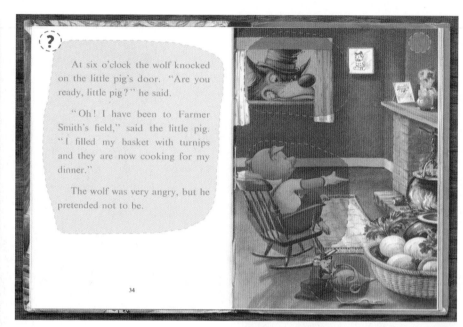

■ In Ladybird Classic Me Books you can tap on words and pictures to record your own audio segments

■ You can purchase a selection of classic books from within the app

Books

Before we owned an iPad, planning our holiday reading could be a bit of a dilemma. We'd need enough books to keep us occupied while lounging on a sunbed for a week or two, but were limited by what we could cram into our suitcase. This reduced our reading list to a few paperbacks. Thanks to today's electronic book apps we can download hundreds of books onto our iPad without eating into our luggage's weight or space allowance! This gives us more than enough material to read on the plane, before bed and on the beach. Indeed the holiday will be over before we can finish our downloaded novels.

When it comes to books there's an app for everyone. You can download your favourite author's

"When it comes to books there's an app for everyone"

latest epic, catch up on the classics for free and keep the tiny tots entertained with illustrated storybooks. There are even comic book apps to keep superhero fans happy!

■ Alice for the iPad contains lots scenes to interact with

■ Share recommendations with avid readers with Goodreads

■ Scan book barcodes and build up your collection

Business

Your iPad isn't just for playing games or reading books – it means Business too! There's a whole category on the App Store dedicated to turning your iPad into a valuable business tool. Time is money, so we've highlighted five essential apps that will speed up typical work chores like quickly recording all of your spontaneous thoughts and ideas and transcribing them into text, creating, editing and sharing Microsoft Word, Excel and PowerPoint files, accessing your office computer desktop from anywhere in the world, viewing and editing PDF files on the move and, thanks to iPads with the two-way cameras, attend important meetings without leaving your home. Our essential apps will enable you to spend less time in the office and more time at play.

"Spend less time in the office and more time at play"

■ Dragon Dictation is a great app for capturing thoughts

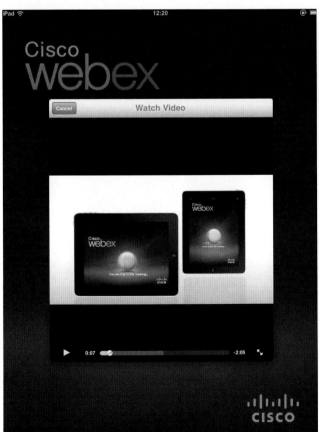
■ WebEx has an introductory video to guide you through the app

■ Dragon Dictation is easy to use – just tap to record

■ With WebEx you can attend virtual board meetings

■ Documents To Go® lets you create and edit all Microsoft Office documents on your iPad

5 essential apps

01 Dragon Dictation Price: Free
Developer: Nuance Communications

You may never have had a personal secretary to type up your words of wisdom, but thanks to this app you can enjoy watching your speech turn to text. Simply tap the record button and chat into your gadget's microphone. If it makes mistakes, then you can summon the keyboard and fine-tune. Once you've created some text then it's a doddle to send it to Facebook or Twitter with a tap. With practise this app could be a genuine time-saver.

02 Documents To Go®
Price: £6.99/$9.99 **Developer:** DataViz, Inc

Anyone who has reservations about trading their laptop in for an iPad should dispel such concerns now because this versatile app allows you to access your Microsoft Office files at any time and view, edit and create new documents on the move. These files can then be transferred wirelessly between your office computer and your device for ease of access and piece of mind while working remotely. Sturdy, reliable and easy to use, this is a sound investment.

03 Wyse PocketCloud Pro
Price: £10.49/$14.99 **Developer:** Wyse Tech

This app is a secure and fast way to remotely connect to your Mac or Windows desktop with your iPad, no matter where you are. Access your files and applications, like Outlook Express, Word, Photoshop, and build your own personal cloud to store all of your important files. It's simple to use and with powerful features, enterprise security and RDP/VNC compatibility, is a great device for helping you work remotely with ease.

04 Cisco WebEx Meetings
Price: Free **Developer:** Cisco

Steer clear of those stuffy boardrooms but never miss a meeting with this great app. With an iPad 2 and later you get two-way video on your device to ensure that you can engage and interact with your colleagues, even if you aren't there in a physical sense.

05 JotNot Scanner Pro
Price: £1.49/$2.99 **Developer:** MobiTech 3000

The benefits of a pocket scanner are plentiful and this app is straightforward enough in its approach. You simply use your iPad camera to scan documents and then email them as JPEGs or PDFs. Ideal for when your printer has run out of paper and you desperately need to file that holiday form.

Essential apps

5 essential apps

01 Fuel Cost

Price: £0.69/$0.99 **Developer:** Daniel Anderton

If you're trying to work out if it's cheaper to drive to a destination or take the train, then this app should help you make an informed choice. You can calculate how many miles your car gets to the gallon and work out the amount of fuel needed for a particular journey. This will help you realise how economical your car is to run. The app supports UK and US measurements and distances so it'll travel well. What's more, it's a universal app so, once paid for, you'll be able to download it for your iPhone too.

02 PocketMoney

Price: £2.99/$3.99 **Developer:** Catamount Soft

In the current economical climate, laying out the small cost for this app will undoubtedly save you cash in the long run as it allows you record and track your finances down to the finest of detail and sync information across all devices. It is an intuitive, feature-rich app that remembers previous transactions and auto-completes them as you begin to type, saving you time and hassle along the way.

03 iCurrency Pad

Price: £0.69/$0.99 **Developer:** Sollico

It's easy to lose out when converting your cash for a trip abroad, but this app's up-to-date exchange rates will help you know when you're getting a good deal. With over 150 currencies to compare you should find what you need, though the Favourites section helpfully narrows down your choice to the most commonly used currencies. The app is slickly designed too, and you can swipe to change a currency with ease.

04 Account Tracker

Price: £1.99/$2.99 **Developer:** Graham Haley

This easy to use accounting app lets you keep track of budgets and expenses and group accounts together with a clear and concise interface. It also includes detailed reports showing balances as well as breakdowns of spending and income. The option to set yourself reminders is also useful for the scattier of brain.

05 Invoice2go for iPad

Price: £10.49/$9.99 **Developer:** Chris Strode

This app provides a quick and easy way to produce and present customers with custom invoices, estimates, bills and reports. With over 20 built-in styles to choose from, there are plenty of templates on offer and you can edit them easily to suit your own needs. If you are self employed then this is a worthy investment.

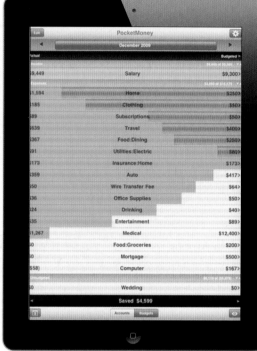

■ Track your finances easily with Pocket Money

Finance

In these tight times it pays to watch your pennies – and you can do that with help from these essential apps from the iTunes Finance category. They will help you avoid being ripped off when converting your currency for a trip abroad or enable you to work out how expensive a road trip will be when filling up your car with petrol. We'll also feature apps designed to help you keep track of your daily expenses, so that you can enjoy spending money while keeping your account safely in the black. There are also apps that allow you to keep up to date with all the latest share prices and read up on all the latest financial news. There is definitely something to suit everyone in the Finance category of the App Store and, by way of a bonus, many of the apps are totally free, which is always helpful.

■ Invoice2go has over 20 built-in styles to choose from

■ The iCurrency app is great for staying within budget

2011-12-19 15:59:38:Expedition 30 Soyuz Rolls to the Pad. SOURCE:NASA IO
Baikonur Cosmodrome, Kazakhstan, Monday, Dec. 19, 2011. The launch of the
Engineer Don Pettit and European Space Agency astronaut and Flight Engine
NASA/Carla Cioffi Mission: International space station For credit and copyrig

Browse All Mode
2011-12-19 : 12 of 1833

■ Learn all about what NASA does with this free app

■ Learn more about the universe with NASA app HD

Education

The iPad is the perfect platform to help you develop your knowledge of a wide range of subjects. Regardless of your age, there's an app to suit everyone. Babies can be stimulated by simple cause and effect when they tap the screen to trigger pictures and relevant sound effects and toddlers can be entertained and educated by story-telling apps that they can interact with by triggering animations with a tap or swipe. Seasoned stargazers can use apps to identify stars and constellations in the night sky or explore the wonders of the universe via images of space captured by the orbiting Hubble telescope. In this section we also recommend good apps to use in the classroom when teaching and apps to enthuse, engage and entertain you when you need a little extra inspiration.

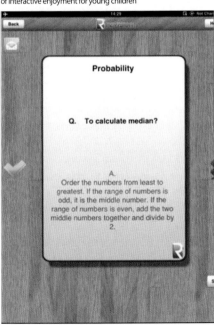
■ The Wheels on the Bus HD app provides plenty of interactive enjoyment for young children

■ Attend engaging and insightful seminars conducted by a wide range of inspiring people with the TED app

■ Prepare for your exams with the Revision App

■ TED holds a plethora of useful talks for you to be informed by

5 essential apps

01 Star Walk for iPad

Price: £2.99/$4.99 **Developer:** Vito Technology

This interstellar app places a Planetarium in your hands. By holding your iPad 2 up against the sky you'll see a computer generated map of the heavens (day or night!). As you scan the heavens, Star Walk overlays graphics that give you extra information. Lines join stars together to indicate constellations, and symbols overlay the relevant stars. The search function pinpoints objects with ease, whether they are distant planets or orbiting satellites.

02 Wheels on the Bus HD

Price: £1.49/$2.99 **Developer:** Duck Duck Moose

This interactive songbook features characters and objects that react to a toddler's tap. As the title song is sung, kids can push the school bus along the screen with their fingers, swipe to open the doors or poke various characters to make them jump! This app will keep your little ones entertained.

03 NASA App HD

Price: Free **Developer:** NASA Ames Research

This free app is an insightful gaze to the stars alongside the NASA space program and includes live streaming of NASA TV, mission information, satellite tracking, Twitter feeds, maps and links to all of the NASA centers and much more. Anyone with even the slightest interest in our solar system would be well advised to check this out as it is well produced with a slick and stylish interface and overflowing with content.

04 TED

Price: Free **Developer:** TED Conferences

This app is a database of insightful, informative talks by some of the world's most influential people across a wide range of fields, the aim being to be enthralled and inspired by experts in the field of economics, technology, agriculture, business and more. Movies can be viewed on iPad or on your TV via AirPlay.

05 Revision App

Price: Free **Developer:** App Giant Ltd

With over one million flash cards and revision notes covering GCSE, A-Level, University and college subjects, this is a great free revision resource to help you get the grades you need. The simple interface makes it easy to revise anywhere and you can easily create your own flash-cards in-app.

Essential apps

Entertainment

Thanks to your ever-present iPad there's no danger that you'll get bored on long journeys (or when sitting on the loo!), especially if you pack it with essential apps from the Entertainment category of the App Store. You can use apps to help you keep tabs on what's on the telly so that you don't miss a thing, or enjoy interactive TV spin-off apps featuring your favourite characters. You can entertain family and friends with a variety of funny or even scary apps. In the following section we'll show you apps that help you record your favourite TV programmes on the move, have fun playing with your photo collection, create professional-looking works of art and see what's on at the cinemas local to where you are (and read up on what's hot and what's pants in the world of cinema). Whatever your entertainment tastes there should be something here to keep you occupied for hours on end.

■ The BBC iPlayer app is great for catching up on missed TV

■ Unleash your inner creativity with Sketchbook Pro

■ Have fun morphing pictures with FaceGoo HD

■ The Sky+ app allows you to record TV on the move

5 essential apps

01 BBC iPlayer
Price: Free
Developer: Media App

This was the original TV catch up viewing portal app released on the iPad and it is still the best. This could be largely thanks to the diverse selection of programmes on offer, which range from insightful documentaries to great comedy and sport, but the interface is so easy to use and well produced that finding things to watch is a quick and easy process.

02 Sketchbook Pro for iPad
Price: £1.49/$1.99
Developer: Autodesk

This app delivers a complete set of sketching and painting tools through a streamlined and intuitive user interface that is based on the professional-grade desktop app, but designed exclusively for the iPad experience. Whether you're a professional illustrator or occasional doodler, this is the perfect app for getting creative.

03 Sky+
Price: Free
Developer: BSkyB

This is an essential app for all Sky+ users as it not only provides full listings for all Sky channels, it also allows you to remotely hit 'record' on your Sky+ box and save what you want, even if you're on the other side of the world. You can also group channel favourites together to create your very own personal TV guide. A great innovative app for Sky users on the go.

04 Podcasts
Price: Free
Developer: iTunes S.a.r.l.

Such is the popularity of podcasts, Apple has migrated the Podcast section out of the iTunes store and into its own app. This works like iBooks and iTunesU in that you can access the Podcast store straight from within the app and then download podcasts to play quickly and easily through the app (you no longer have to switch to your Music app).

05 FaceGoo HD
Price: £1.99/$2.99
Developer: Robot Wheelie

This fun, distracting app lets you manipulate and morph pictures in to grotesque parodies. You can use the preloaded portraits or import your own images and the effects that you can apply with your fingers are incredible – simply swipe your finger to start distorting and apply all manner of scars and boils.

5 essential apps

01 FIFA 13
Price: £4.99/$6.99
Developer: EA Swiss S.a.r.l.

 It is only now that the iPad is becoming a viable alternative to the PS3 and Xbox 360 as a gaming machine – especially football games. But FIFA 13 has improved most aspects since last year's outing, notably the controls, which are noticeably more responsive. And it makes a big different to how close you now feel to the action. Of course, the amount of teams and leagues is always a bonus!

02 World Of Goo HD
Price: £2.99/$4.99
Developer: 2D BOY

 This quirky puzzle game has you pulling and plying balls of goo to shape structures and defences to conquer the many levels. This cute, curious game is brimming with personality and features some stunning visual effects. The game also features a massive online competition where goo-getters battle on a live leaderboard to build the tallest tower of goo. Fun for all the family.

03 Angry Birds HD
Price: £1.99/$2.99
Developer: Chillingo Ltd

 This entertaining platform and puzzle game deserves a place on every iPad. Use a catapult to fire a variety of birds through the air to topple objects and kill enemies hiding behind them. Different birds have different abilities – tap on a bird to make it speed up or even explode. Be warned – its combination of addictive play and high production values can eat your spare time up.

04 Plants Vs Zombies HD
Price: £4.99/$6.99
Developer: PopCap Games

 This tower defense game has you protecting your home against multiple waves of shambling zombies. You'll have to act fast and plan ahead to keep them from your door while using sunlight to fuel your fauna army. As you progress you'll unlock new wacky plants to line-up and delay or disintegrate the decaying hordes. Just brilliant.

05 Order & Chaos© Online
Price: £4.99/$6.99
Developer: Gameloft

 This is the iPad's premier real-time full 3D MMORPG that places players into a graphically-rich and diverse fantasy world to play alongside thousands of other adventurers. You can lose yourself in this for weeks on end. You are provided with a three-month subscription upon download but after that you pay to play.

Games

The iPad is a gamer's dream come true. Its high-quality screen displays pixels perfectly so you can enjoy a game's colours and graphics to the full. It's more than capable of pushing pixels around at a decent frame rate so the action never falters. Unlike traditional handheld consoles, iPad games are relatively cheap (or even free for lite 'try before you buy' versions), so you'll never be short of games to enjoy. Gameplay varies dramatically, from first-person shooters to exhilarating sports platform games. The iPad's touch screen makes it possible to play games without a joypad – and many apps make good use of this feature. Some games also put the iPad's accelerometer to good use so that you can steer characters by simply tilting the device. Whatever style of game you favour there's sure to be something to take your fancy in our essential roundup, right here.

■ Even life in the distant reaches of the galaxy have played Angry Birds

■ Plants Vs Zombies is insanely addictive

■ Take your fight online with Order & Chaos© Online

■ FIFA 13 – now more responsive than ever

Essential apps

Health & Fitness

We all make plans to stay fitter and thinner at various times (especially in the new year with resolutions to be made), though our motivation often runs out of steam. However, with the right apps on your iPad you should be able to see a real change in your fitness level each day. For starters there are apps designed to help you to record and reduce your calorie intake, enabling you to lose weight at a pace that suits you, as well as highlighting flaws in your current diet. We'll even show you how to turn your iPad into high-tech barcode scanner that reads the amount of calories in the food you intend to buy and tells you if it's healthy or not. In case of accidents you can turn to apps for advice, and perform life-saving first aid if necessary. Need a symptom diagnosed? There is an app for that too. Needless to say our essential apps will provide you with guidance and advice, but they're no substitute for seeking a professional in a medical emergency. Here we recommend a great selection of apps for staying in shape and learning more about your body.

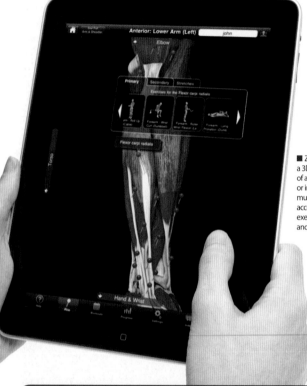

■ Zoom in on a 3D diagram of a body part or individual muscle to access specific exercises and more

■ Fitness for iPad lets you track your food intake

■ Get fit with the Fitness for iPad app's help

5 essential apps

01 Fitness for iPad
Price: £0.69/$0.99
Developer: Arawella Corp

This feature-heavy app provides you with hundreds of fitness exercises and yoga poses, 40 complete workouts, a calorie counter, body tracker and plenty of extra tools for helping you get into shape and monitor your fitness. It is a friendly, informative app that is easy to follow and packed with information to help you keep in shape. The price is very enticing too.

02 Army Survival for iPad/iPhone
Price: £1.49/$2.99
Developer: Double Dog

This digital field manual is the most authoritative survival guide available on iPad and comes packed with over 1,400 pages rammed with tricks of the trade for staying alive while out in the wild. This is a fascinating and insightful read that is well-presented and easy-to-follow thanks to neat diagrams and plenty of information across a wide range of topics.

03 Food Scanner: Good Food or Bad Food?
Price: £0.69/$0.99
Developer: Arawella Corp

If you're into healthy eating and treat your body like a temple, this app is designed to help you make informed choices on what you eat. Simply use the cameras on your iPad 2 scan the barcodes on food and the app determines if it's good or bad for you. Okay so it's a big part gimmick, but it's still a useful app that is great for showing off your device while helping up stay in shape.

04 iMuscle – (NOVA Series) – iPad Edition
Price: £1.49/$2.99
Developer: 3D4Medical.com

Through this app you can identify a body part or individual muscle by zooming in on a 3D diagram of the human body and then access a host of exercises associated with the development or rehabilitation of that particular muscle. It's a great tool as a teaching aid for fitness instructors and is an impressively detailed app.

05 Quit Smoking Now HD
Price: £4.99/$6.99
Developer: Craig Ray

If determined to beat the demon weed then this app provides hypnotherapy treatment from Max Kirsten that is proven to get results. Kirsten is renowned and highly qualified in the field and counts many celebrities as clients, including the actor Ewan McGregor, who professes to have given up thanks to this very download, and so can you!

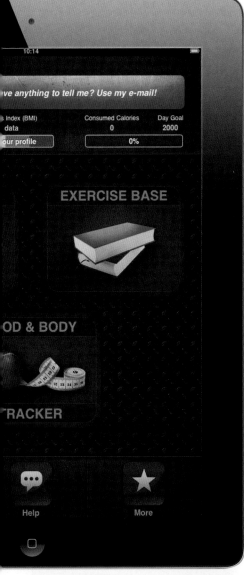
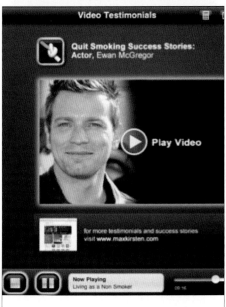

■ Kick the habit once and for all with Quit Smoking Now HD

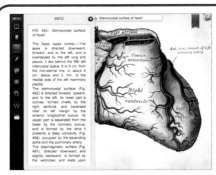

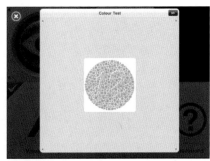

■ The Grays Anatomy app is packed with medical insight and is a great learning aid for students

■ Test your eyes for free with the Vision Test app

Medical

The Medical category of the App Store contains apps that complement the ones in the Health & Fitness section, so you're spoiled for choice when it comes to finding apps to help you stay fit and well. Some of the best apps in this category are detailed and insightful reference guides that will prove invaluable for medical students and anyone working in the field of medicine, but there is also a very wide selection of self-help aids to monitor blood pressure, units of alcohol, sugar levels and so on – so if you suffer from a particular affliction, then you're sure to find an app that will help you monitor and cope with your condition. There are also some very good eye-testing apps available that let you assess your peepers in the comfort of your own home to determine if you should get yourself down to the opticians for a proper test.

■ The Medical – Oxford Dictionary app is expensive, but worth it

5 essential apps

01 Vision Test

Price: Free **Developer:** 3 Sided Cube Design

If you have a somewhat casual approach to getting your eyes tested regularly then Vision Test is a decent gauge for testing if your peepers are in need of a professional examination. It includes a Visual Acuity Test, Astigmatism Test, Duochrome Test, Colour Test and Far Field Vision Test, as well as an optician finder, advice and facts and a quiz to test your knowledge. It's totally free too!

02 Grays Anatomy Premium

Price: £1.99/$2.99 **Developer:** Luke Allen

First published in 1858 and considered by many to the one of the most iconic and significant medical books of all time, Grays Anatomy is now available on the iPad and grabs the technology with both hands to present its information in engaging new ways, accompanied by high-resolution images. It's a great, insightful source of information that will be invaluable to trainee doctors and nurses.

03 Medical – Oxford Dictionary

Price: £10.49/$15.99
Developer: Handmark, Inc

This illustrated dictionary contains 12,500 authoritative entries on all aspects of medical science and is complimented by over 140 illustrations. Written and updated regularly by a dedicated team of medical experts, this is a great reference app for all things medical related that will prove invaluable to medical students and anyone working in medicine.

04 The Human Body

Price: £2.99/$4.99 **Developer:** Amber Books

A very cool app that describes 300 parts of the human anatomy through detailed illustrations and annotations. Each entry can be zoomed in on for extra scrutiny and the expert writers keep the info concise and accessible. A worthwhile and cheaper alternative to the wealth of in-depth references guides available.

05 The Fat Finger

Price: £1.49/$2.99 **Developer:** Robert DiGiacomo

Designed to provide a clean, fun and easy-to-use interface with clear and easy-to-understand voices, this app will benefit individuals with visual problems or fine motor difficulties. You simply select a photo and a clear voice will read your phrase aloud. All of the phrases are fully customisable and you can add anything.

Essential apps

5 essential apps

01 The Photo Cookbook

Price: £2.99/$4.99 **Developer:** ditter. projektagentur Gmb

The Photo Cook Book – Quick and Easy does what it says on the tin! If you want to develop some culinary skills, then the lavishly illustrated Photo Cookbook is a must have. This educational app is packed full of recipes that guide you step-by-step. There's a wide range of dishes and desserts to create. You can also refer to a photo of a meal's raw ingredients when you're out shopping, so that you don't miss a thing!

02 Tesco Food

Price: Free **Developer:** Tesco PLC

This fine free app provides plenty of culinary inspiration and allows you to purchased and get delivered all the ingredients you need to make your feast of fancy. The app is quick and easy to use and you can store all of the recipes that you like as favourites to access later and the app will sync to your computer, so you can start shopping for ingredients on one device and then continue on another.

03 eBay for iPad

Price: Free **Developer:** eBay Inc

If you're a keen eBay user then this app is all you need to keep track of your online auctions. It's formatted for your iPad screen, so whether you're buying or selling you can find the information you need with ease. It can be a chore to leave feedback on multiple auctions or mark items as having been dispatched. Thanks to this fab app you can perform these tedious tasks on the move and stay on top of your eBay admin.

04 AroundMe

Price: Free **Developer:** Tweakersoft

Every iPad needs an app that displays local amenities, and this one does the job effectively. Scroll through a list of categories (like Parking) and see a list of all the options (with the closest listed first). A quick tap will show the location on a map in relation to your own position.

05 Groupon HD

Price: Free **Developer:** Groupon, Inc

Groupon is a good source for the best deals on things to do, stuff to eat, places to visit, hotels to frequent and more. The latest deals close to your location are listed with heavy discounts and you can opt to take up an offer and order it through the app. The offers are nice and diverse and using the app is easy.

Lifestyle

The Lifestyle category of the App Store contains apps covering a diverse range of subjects. If you're keen on getting out and about (whether that's through walking or cycling), then you can use apps to map your favourite routes and discover how long a particular journey is in miles. While on a stroll you can fire up apps to help you discover local amenities (like pubs or restaurants), or check out the status of your eBay auctions when you're on the move. If you want to conquer your lack of cooking skills then we have a must-have app that will enable you to impress family and friends with newfound cooking skills and shop for essential ingredients (or pretty much anything else, for that matter). Whatever your lifestyle, you are sure to find apps that will make a difference to how you live your life.

"Whatever lifestyle, these apps should make a difference"

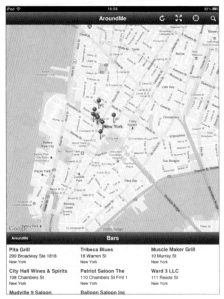

■ Discover the world around you with AroundMe

■ The eBay app is great for shopping and completing fiddly admin on the move

■ The Groupon app provides a daily selection of interesting and enticing offers

■ Rustle up something special for dinner with the Tesco Food app

5 essential apps

01 Bloom HD
Price: £2.49/$3.99
Developer: Opal Limited

 A hypnotic, ambient app in which you create sound patterns by tapping different parts of the screen. It works brilliantly and you can create some great-sounding multi-layered pieces of music within minutes thanks to the simple interface. Developed by ambient pioneer Brian Eno and musician Peter Chivers, the quality shines through.

02 djay
Price: £6.99/$10.99
Developer: algoriddim

 This app is amazing – it looks lovely and functions fabulously. It places two vinyl turntables on your iPad's screen. You can place tracks from your iTunes library onto each turntable and play the tracks as if they were vinyl. A fader enables you to mix the two records together to create something new. You can mix live, or record and share your mix with mates.

03 Björk: Biophilia
Price: £8.99/$14.99
Developer: Second Wind Ltd

 So engaging that it has been adopted as part of the school curriculum in Björk's native Reykjavik, Biophilia is an innovative multimedia exploration of music, nature and technology. Comprising of a full suite of original music and interactive, educational artworks, Biophilia is released as ten in-app experiences that are accessed through a 3D galaxy. Definitely a one-off.

04 Shazam for iPad
Price: Free
Developer: Shazam Entertainment Ltd.

 Hear a song you like but have no idea which band performs it? With Shazam you can whip out your iPad, let it listen to the music and identify the track in moments. You can discover song lyrics, see album covers and download the track via iTunes. This is definitely a musical must have for every iPad user with an interest in the latest tunes.

05 Amplitube for iPad
Price: £13.99/$16.99
Developer: IK Multimedia US, LLC

Used in conjunction with the iRig interface adaptor, AmpliTube allows you to transform your iPad into a feature-heavy electric guitar amp by plugging in your guitar and utilising a host of pedal effects. Brilliant if you can't afford a Marshall, this is one way to keep the neighbours happy.

Music

If you love listening to music, or even want to make it, then the following essential apps deserve a place on your iPad. We'll feature an amazing app that enables you to mix the Music library's tracks together like an old-school DJ (complete with scratchy back spins that you can produce by swiping the iPad's screen!). Alternatively you may want to simply stroke the screen to generate synthesized sounds and create a relaxing ambient soundscape – there's an app for that too! If you'd rather consume music than create it, then there's an app that will tell you the track and artist that you're listening to by sampling it through your iPad's mic, so you won't miss out on discovering new bands. You can rediscover old music too by listening to music-streaming apps, and turn your iPad into a radio that will pick up (and even record) stations from anywhere in the world.

■ Go on a fantastic voyage of discovery with Björk

■ Shazam will have no trouble identifying songs for you to buy

■ Make sweet sounds with the easy-to-use Bloom HD app

■ Become a virtual DJ in the clever djay app

Essential apps

5 essential apps

01 CoPilot Live Premium HD

Price: £34.99/$49.99 **Developer:** ALK Technologies, LTD.

 This is the most expensive app in our feature, but it's much cheaper than buying a dedicated satnav. It uses your iPad's GPS function to help you navigate road trips. Like other satnav displays, you can see your vehicle's position on a 3D map and follow arrows that guide you. When you get to complex junctions a lane indicator keeps you on track. It's worth buying a hands-free mount holder so you don't get distracted holding your gadget.

02 Layar Reality Browser

Price: Free **Developer:** Layar B.V.

 Instead of using a 2D map to find local points of interest, try a bit of augmented reality! Layar works by allowing you to search for a particular amenity (like a coffee shop). Instead of displaying the search results as icons on a 2D map it overlays them on your iPad 2's live camera image. As you pan the device to view a location you'll see floating icons or images that represent the locations of your search results.

03 Trails – GPS tracker

Price: £2.49/$3.99 **Developer:** Felix Lamouroux

If you're a big fan of hiking then this app will let you record your adventures using the iPad's GPS facility. You can snap photos of interesting sights along the way and create waypoints to mark points of interest. Cyclists should find this app useful to as it can display the topography of the terrain. You can also download maps before you set out in case the iPad can't get a signal on your journey.

04 ForeverMap

Price: £1.49/$2.99 **Developer:** skobbler GmbH

If you're travelling abroad it can cost a fortune to download map details using the standard Maps app. ForeverMap lets you download a country or city's map before you travel so you can avoid excessive data roaming charges. You can then use the downloaded map to plan routes and discover points of interest.

05 Plane Finder HD

Price: £4.99/$6.99 **Developer:** pinkfroot limited

 This fascinating real-time plane-tracking app is a real eye-opener, as you can see just how full our skies are with aircraft. If your friends or family are travelling by air you can follow their progress by searching for their flight number. An essential app for any flight enthusiast. There's a cut-down free version available too.

Navigation

We tend to carry our iPad around with us at all times, so it's the perfect device to help us get where we want to go, or find local amenities like pubs or hotels. Your iPad already comes with a decent built-in Maps app that does a great job of showing you how to get from A to B – but there are other apps that can extend and expand your gadget's navigational abilities in exciting ways. In this section we'll introduce you to five essential navigation apps that perform a variety of different functions. One of them even transforms your iPad into a turn-by-turn navigator at the fraction of the price of a dedicated gadget like a TomTom satnav – just make sure you use it safely in the car. You can also keep tabs on the flight paths of specific planes, or discover the location of local points of interest by panning the iPad 2's camera around the area you are in.

■ ForeverMap could save you a lot of money while you're travelling

■ Zoom in and out of ForeverMap with a pinch

■ Discover what's in the sky above your head with the Plane Finder HD app

■ In the 3D view CoPilot shows you which turn to take to get home safely

News

If you're hungry for the latest news then the iPad is the perfect gadget to sate your appetite. We all have different interests when it comes to news, so there are specialist apps for every genre of news – like the world of science fiction for example. Most newspapers have an online edition, but that can be a fiddle to navigate using your iPad's Safari browser. We'll take a look at a couple of the best iPad newspaper apps to help you enjoy a decent digital version of your favourite newspaper without having to pinch to zoom in on small web browser text. There are even apps that will turn your iPad into a newsreader, so you can listen to headlines from any news source you choose while on the move. There's even an app that enables you to stream your favourite podcasts straight to your iPad without you having to download and sync them. The iPad offers so much in the way of news, you're guaranteed to stay informed.

"There are specialist apps for every genre of news"

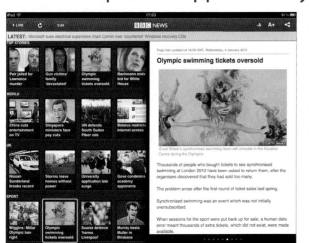

■ News is broken up into helpful headlines that you can explore in a tap

■ The BBC News app lets you watch events however you want

■ Turn pages, zoom in – Flipboard makes catching up on news quick and stylish

■ Browse through topics via category or search for something in the Guardian

■ The Guardian Newsstand app is well presented and ideal for iPad use

5 essential apps

01 The Guardian

Price: Free **Developer:** Guardian News and Media Limited

 This is the digital edition of the popular *Guardian* newspaper. Although the app is free to download you'll need to pay £3.99 for a 12-month subscription. Headlines are grouped under sections like Top stories or World news. All the stories are cross-referenced, making it easy to discover more information about an event. If you've a Wi-Fi connection there are video clips and podcasts to stream. There's a customisable dock where you can store links to your favourite features.

02 BBC News

Price: Free **Developer: Media Applications**

Through this app you can get all the latest breaking news from the BBC and its global network of journalists delivered in an attractive and engaging interface. Stories are arranged in categories, including Top Stories, UK News and World News and cover a wide range of topics, including world news, politics, technology and sport. The app also offers the BBC News Channel streamed live, plus social features.

03 Sky News

Price: Free **Developer:** BSkyB

A well-presented and easily accessible app that places all the latest breaking news into your hands and allows you to decide what you want to watch and how you want to watch it. Includes live feeds and in-depth reports and analysis, plus a timeline that allows you to follow the day's events and unravel key moments in the past 24 hours. The best feature is the ability to rewind news feeds so you never miss a story.

04 Blastr

Price: Free **Developer:** NBC Universal, Inc.

If you're a science-fiction fan then Blastr is a useful way to beam stories and images from a variety of SF genres straight to your iPad. You can browse for stories via Sections like Horror or Rumors, or scroll through the latest news in chronological order. Just watch out for those spoilers.

05 Flipboard

Price: Free **Developer:** Flipboard, Inc

 If you only have a limited timespan to fish for news on the web then Flipboard is here to help. The app lavishly lays out all of your social shares and news feeds in an easy to peruse magazine format, so you can get one massive news hit in a fraction of the time.

Essential apps

5 essential apps

01 Aelios Weather
Price: £2.99/$4.99
Developer: Jime

 If you are the sort of person who travels around a lot then this is a lavishly-produced app to help you track the weather all over the planet. You can jump to any country by moving and pinching maps, get 24-hour forecasts that update regularly and seven-day forecasts to help you plan ahead. It also looks fantastic, which doesn't harm its appeal at all. Perfect.

02 Weather HD
Price: £1.49/$2.99
Developer: vimov, LLC

 This app isn't as informative as some of the others, but it's the prettiest to look at. The current weather conditions are represented using colourful HD videos. Clouds float by, raindrops fall or the Sun rises over windblown wheat stalks. This enables the app to function as attractive moving wallpaper. There's also text to inform you of temperature, humidity and wind strength.

03 Aero Weather Pro
Price: £2.49/$3.99
Developer: Pascal Dreer

 Thanks to AeroWeather Pro you can get current and precise weather conditions, as well as forecasts, which are used by pilots for their flight preparations. You can choose worldwide airport weather stations from the built-in database by either name of ICAO code and data will be shown in its original format or fully decoded into easy-to-understand texts.

04 Moon Calendar
Price: £0.69/$0.99
Developer: Rivolu Pte Ltd

This app lets you understand and track the movements of our moon. It provides plenty of lunar insight including when you can expect new moons, full moons or even find out when the sun will rise in your location. Everything is presented in a great-looking interface and it's easy to use, making this the perfect app for lunar gazers everywhere.

05 Weather+
Price: £0.69/$0.99
Developer: International Travel Weather Calculator

 If you need a weather forecast in a hurry then this app places all you need to know on a single screen. Various widgets give you time, temperature, humidity and wind strength. You can customise the screen to simplify it, so only the most useful information is visible against the background.

Weather

Most of us will just want an app that forecasts the weather in our area for the next few days – and there are plenty of apps that perform that function very well.

We have trawled through the App Store for apps that will bring you a wide range of weather-related information. There's a deluge of weather-centric apps to choose from, which can make it a challenge to find which apps are essential (and which actually work!). When choosing our five essential apps we have gone for variety, to make sure that all your weather-related needs will be covered. You'll then know when to reach for the umbrella or a tube of suntan lotion.

We've gone for apps that display the forecasts as attractive weather-themed videos, apps that display satellite cloud maps plus apps that give you more specialist forecasts like pollen counts. Ultimately, we suspect that you'll only ever need one decent weather app, but here are five anyway!

■ Get sleek and stylish updates with Aero Weather

■ Aelios Weather draws its information from a wealth of trusted sources for you to get the best weather insight as you can

■ Aelios Weather present the weather where you are in a sleek and stylish manner

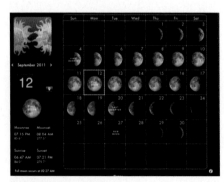
■ Monitor the movements of the moon with the aptly named Moon Calendar app

■ Aero Weather makes it easy to share your current climate with other people

Photography

Thanks to your ever-present iPad 2 and new iPad, there's no danger that you'll miss a photo (or video) opportunity. The built-in Camera app enables you to focus on your subject matter and capture a decent exposure much of the time, but there will be occasions when you may want to produce more creative-looking results. Some of our essential apps enable you to turn photos into striking works of art or paintings at the touch of a button, so you can impress your friends with your apparent artistic skills. Another of our essential apps gives you a wide range of filters to play around with, turning ordinary snapshots into extraordinary retro images with attractive borders, amongst many other fancy effects. There's even an app to compliment and improve your Photoshop productivity while on the move. If you're into photography then you'll find thousands of products on the App Store to help you unleash your inner creativity and produce stunning photos that you'll want to show off.

■ Manage and edit your images with the intuitive iPhoto app

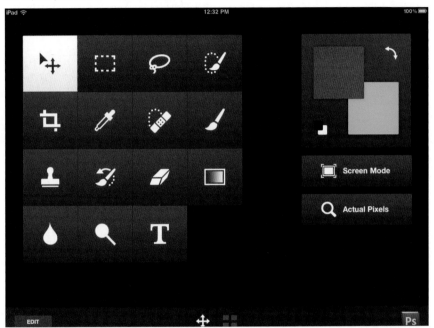

■ Adobe® Nav is an excellent tool to use to edit your images while on the move

■ Create stunning images with Filterstorm

5 essential apps

01 Photogene for iPad
Price: £1.99/$2.99
Developer: Omer Shoor

Photogene is a photo-editing app that is packed full of fun features to make the process enthralling rather than a chore. Included in the package are tools to help you crop and straighten images, adjust the colours, reduce red-eye and apply special effects such as reflection and vignette. You can also get arty on your pictures by applying filters, text boxes and frames.

02 Filterstorm
Price: £2.49/$3.99
Developer: Tai Shimizu

Using a uniquely crafted touch interface, Filterstorm allows for more intuitive editing than its desktop counterparts with a toolset designed for serious photography. Ideal for photography professionals or any who wants to get the most out of their pictures, this app presents a varied toolset and allows you to create and apply artistic brilliance.

03 Strip Designer
Price: £1.99/$2.99
Developer: Jens Egeblad

This app, as the name somewhat suggests,allows you to turn your photographs into comic strips. By selecting one of the many included templates you simply import your images and style them up by cropping, angling and applying speech bubbles and captions. It's great fun and will help you craft and tell stories through photos.

04 Adobe® Nav for Photoshop®
Price: £1.49/$2.99
Developer: Adobe Systems

This companion app provides a whole new way to interact with Photoshop CS5 on your computer. Transfer images from you iPad directly to Photoshop and use it to select and browse through open Photoshop documents while on the move. This, along with other Adobe apps such as Eazel and Color Lava make mobile artwork easy,

05 iPhoto
Price: £2.99/$4.99
Developer: iTunes S.a.r.l.

Through this universal app, you can browse, edit and share your photos straight from your iPad. You can touch and drag on the parts of the image that you want to change and use a face-aware crop tool to keep your friends and family in the picture whenever you change the aspect ratio. A fun and engaging app to use.

Essential apps

5 essential apps

01 2Do
Price: £6.99/$9.99 **Developer:** Guided Ways Technologies Ltd

One way to keep organised is to write a list and cross tasks out as they're done. Unlike some free apps, 2Do enables you to group various tasks into different calendars. You can also prioritise tasks so that the most urgent ones are at the top. You can even assign notes and pictures and add practical actions that let you call or mail a contact in a click. Add an alarm and you'll receive a notification when it needs to be done.

02 Dropbox
Price: Free **Developer:** Dropbox

There are plenty of file-sharing apps, but Dropbox stands out from the crowd. The free service gives you a Dropbox folder on your computer and one on your iPad. When you drag a file into your computer's Dropbox it's automatically uploaded to an online folder, enabling you to view the file using the iPad. You can pay to increase the 2GB storage capacity. A fast and effective file-sharing app.

03 Keynote
Price: £6.99/$9.99 **Developer:** Apple

Keynote is a powerful presentation tool that has been on the Mac for a while, but with this iPad edition you can carry on working while on the move, now by syncing with iCloud too. Cleverly using the iPad's touch interface, the app allows you to choose from templates, create sophisticated animations and much more. Well worth a purchase.

04 Pages
Price: £6.99/$9.99 **Developer:** Apple, Inc

Anyone unsure of ditching their laptop in favour of an iPad need only look at Pages. This app is a versatile desktop publishing app that lets you create professional-looking page designs in minutes. With an intuitive set of tools, plenty of tutorials and templates, you can instantly create eye-catching letters, reports, flyers, cards, posters and more and customise them easily.

05 Google Drive
Price: Free **Developer:** Google, Inc

This is another free cloud service that lets you create, share and keep all of your files in one place. You are provided with 5GB of space to use and once your files are uploaded, you can access them from anywhere – including other iOS devices, Macs or any computer with a web browser. Fast and convenient.

■ Create your own posters, fliers, brochures… pretty much whatever you want in the brilliant Pages app

Productivity

Thanks to apps, your iPad can be many things. It has the power to become a communications device, a camera or even a games console. It can also help you get things done in the home or in your office thanks to a range of essential Productivity apps. In this section we'll show you apps that enable you to access (and even share) important documents while you're out of the office, so you're no longer chained to your desk. If you're a MobileMe user then you can access your iDisk from your iPad too even use your device to create wonderfully stylish pages and documents that will really command attention. Of course, we couldn't fail to include some quality personal organiser apps – mainly because there are just so many on the App Store that they're almost impossible to overlook. Here's a run down of those essential productivity apps to get your iPad working for you.

■ With Dropbox you can transfer files with an incredible amount of ease

Learn more about Pages
Scroll through the document. Touch the images and text. And experience the most powerful word processor ever made for a mobile device.

■ The Pages app on the iPad is a great tool that lets you create a variety of things while on the move

Reference

We all take the internet for granted as a source of information, and the iPad is often the portal we use when we need to access the world wide web's ocean of knowledge. Although the Safari app's Google search field is often our first port of call looking for information, it can take a while to wade through hundreds of results before we find what we're after. The apps featured in this section should help you narrow down your search to find relevant information more quickly, whether it's crime statistics for your hometown or the missing link in your family tree. We've also included the obligatory augmented reality app, so that you can discover what's out there in the universe above our heads through the iPad 2's camera! Our essential reference apps should help you filter your search for information more effectively.

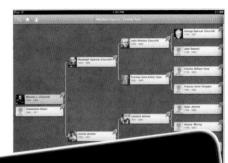
■ Browse your family trees while on the move in Ancestry

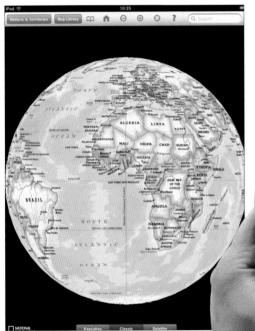
■ Play with the globe in World Atlas HD

■ Explore our planet with World Atlas HD's map

5 essential apps

01 World Atlas HD
Price: £0.69/$0.99
Developer: acrossair

 Designed specifically for iPad, National Geographic's new and improved World Atlas HD app puts the best, most detailed maps into the palm of your hand. You can jump to anywhere in the world instantly and grab all kinds of facts and insight about the countries you tap on. You can also learn all abut the flags and cultures.

02 Airports
Price: £3.99/$5.99
Developer: Peter Lundkvist

 This is an insightful and enthralling app for anyone interested in aviation. A quick search function lets you find airports by city, name, ICAO or IATA code and the app comes bulging with a wide range of data, including the dimensions and surface type of each runway, time zone, sunrise/sunset times and ATIS frequencies. The perfect app for plane spotters.

03 The Night Sky
Price: £0.69/$0.99
Developer: iCandi Apps

 This app enables you to see the stars, planets and satellites just by standing there and holding your device up to the night sky. All names of the stars and other objects will then be presented on your screen in real-time. It's a truly magical app that is great for showing off your device to friends and engaging and enthralling children keen to learn about the stars.

04 Brian Cox's Wonders of the Universe
Price: £4.99/$6.99
Developer: Harper Collins Publishers Limited

 Cox has always been an engaging teacher whose infectious enthusiasm could doubtless rustle up interest in any subject. But here he has a great app to back him up that lets you journey through our Solar System, hopping off onto all of the moons and planets along the way.

05 Ancestry
Price: Free
Developer: Ancestry.com

If you're investigating your family tree then chances are you'll be a member of Ancestry.com. This app formats that site for your iPad, enabling you to view or edit trees with ease and even upload photos of family heirlooms. This well-designed app provides an easy way to share family trees with relatives.

Essential apps

Social networking

Many of us spend more time socialising online than we do in the flesh, enabling us to sustain friendships with family, friends and colleagues over any distance. Your ever-present iPad is a key tool in helping you keep up-to-date with your online friends. We'll take a look at apps that let you find out who's doing what, and discover apps to communicate, free of charge, with other iPad users. If you use any of

the main social networking sites then you'll find dedicated apps that let you access these sites with ease. We'll take a look at the apps from big-hitters like Facebook and Twitter, and show you ways to gather different networks into a single app. As well as keeping up with the social whirl we'll also show you an app that allow you to add even more personality to your tweets too.

■ Twitter has now been integrated in iOS 6 to make it easier than ever to tweet away

■ After a long wait, Facebook now has its own dedicated iPad app

■ Stay in your social loop with ease thanks to the intuitive IM+ app

■ With the Facebook app it is now even easier to stay in touch with friends and share your photos

5 essential apps

01 IM+
Price: Free **Developer:** SHAPE Services

The problem with keeping track of your mates is that they may be scattered across a variety of social networking sites. Fortunately you can gather everyone together using IM+. This app is an all-in-one messenger that enables you to see who's online regardless of their preferred social network This could become your one-stop-shop when it comes to social network chats.

02 Skype for iPad
Price: Free **Developer:** Skype Software S.a.r.l

Skype is an amazing app that lets you voice, text and video chat with friends who also have Skype installed on their laptop or iPhone. It does this for free, making it an essential social networking app for any iPad 2. You can also make low cost calls to overseas landlines by buying Skype credits. These can automatically be updated via a feed from your PayPal account, so there's no danger of the call becoming interrupted.

03 SoundCloud
Price: Free **Developer:** SoundCloud Ltd

SoundCloud is a social network… for sounds. You can upload you own tracks and samples, borrow new sounds from fellow users and follow established artists who regularly provide a sneaky pre-release heads-up on their new projects. The community is enthusiastic and welcoming and you will find everyone from the Smashing Pumpkins' Billy Corgan to Doctor from Doctor And The Medics onboard.

04 Facebook
Price: Free **Developer:** Facebook, Inc.

With more than 6 million active users we probably don't need to tell you that Facebook is a popular social networking site, but if you're a Facebook addict then this app must be included on your iPad. Update your Facebook status via your iPad and even let people keep tabs on your recent GPS locations.

05 Twitter
Price: Free **Developer:** Twitter, Inc

Do we need to tell you what Twitter is? Well, if you're back from outer space then Twitter is a site that lets you announce (or tweet) your current activity or opinion in 140 characters or less. You can tweet, or follow other users' tweets. A great way to snoop on the daily lives of others.

5 essential apps

01 i-Drills Soccer
Price: £4.99/$6.99
Developer: Selesti Limited

If you are a football coach and in need of inspiration for new training drills in order to keep your players sharp, then this app has loads to download for free that includes all aspects of the game, such as attacking, defending, set-pieces and more. It's a little rough around the edges and in need of an update but, until now, is the best we've found.

02 Bike Repair HD
Price: £2.49/$3.99
Developer: Atomic Softwares

Cycling can be a great way to stay fit, but if you have mechanical problems it can be expensive. Buying this app could save you a bob or two as it shows you how to diagnose and fix common faults. Solve a problem by tapping on the appropriate part. Scroll through the list of possible problems and see an illustrated step-by-step guide on how to fix the fault.

03 Sky Sports News
Price: Free
Developer: BSkyB

This sleek, well-designed app is rammed with content – from insight and opinion to all the latest scores, behind the scenes news and sports results. An essential download for any self-confessed sports freak, it is a great, stylish way to get all the latest sports news in a format that is easy to navigate and digest on your iPad. Another great app from Sky, then…

04 Golfshot: Golf GPS
Price: £13.99/$19.99
Developer: Shotzoom Soft

You will need a 3G iPad to get the most out of this app, but it features a handy GPS rangefinder with distances to the front, center and back of the green, up to 40 professionally-mapped targets per hole and much more. So if you want to navigate your way around the course and ensure that you never lose your ball, then this is the perfect app for you.

05 NHL GameCenter 2011-2012 Premium
Price: Free
Developer: NHL Interactive

If you're into hockey then this app comes packed with scores, stats, photos and more. If you upgrade to the Premium edition in-app then you also get access to a live game radio, video highlights and picks of the week. Perfect for the armchair fan, we wish more sports had this.

Sports

There are many sports and recreational activities to enjoy, so no matter what sport you're interested in, there's bound to be an app for you in our sporting must haves. We have an app that enables cyclists to save repair bills by diagnosing mechanical problems and showing them the solutions. If you're aspiring to be the next 'Special One' then there are loads of decent coaching apps available that cater for a wide range of sports, including CoachPad, that makes creating your own training exercises a breeze. We have also picked out the best app for up-to-the-minute sports news, a useful app for improving your golf and we take a look at the ultimate app for the armchair ice hockey fan, which is so good that we wish other sports would follow suit and emulate the format. So, as you can see, the wonderful world of sport is well served on iPad.

■ Teaching made easy with i-Drills Soccer

■ Get up-to-the-minute sports updates thanks to Sky Sports News

■ Everything you need to know about ice hockey in NHL GameCenter

■ The Sky Sports News app has videos you can watch while on the move

Essential apps

5 essential apps

01 Kayak

Price: Free **Developer:** Kayak Software Corp

As a travel app, Kayak is a good all-rounder. It enables you to find the cheapest flight and hotel prices from the comfort of your iPad's screen. Before heading off use its tickbox packing list to ensure that you don't forget important things. It's also a useful app when starting your journey too, as the Flight Tracker option enables you to see if you plane is going to take off as scheduled. There's even a currency converter. A traveller's must have!

02 TripAdvisor

Price: Free **Developer:** TripAdvisor LLC

Holidays can be expensive and you don't get many of them, so you'll want them to be perfect. This app enables you to read reviews of hotels and restaurants from people who've already experienced them. The Things to do section is very useful as it will give you advice about various tourist attractions without the need to fork out for a guidebook. An informative travel app.

03 Wikihood for iPad

Price: Free **Developer:** Dr Stephan Gillmeier

Wikipedia is a dauntingly large resource. Fortunately, this clever app helps you mine that mass of information to bring you interesting local knowledge. Discover nearby points of interest and read articles on famous people with a local connection. You can also view photos attached to Wikipedia entries, so no matter how long you've lived in an area you're sure to learn something new about it.

04 FlightTrack

Price: £2.99/$4.99 **Developer:** Ben Kazez

If you are a frequent flyer then this app provides all of the departure info, delay alerts and gate numbers you will ever need. Full international coverage means that you can track all of your flights worldwide find alternate flights in the event of a cancellation.

05 Google Earth

Price: Free **Developer:** Google, Inc

Still free and still kicking ass, Google Earth is a fascinating and engrossing app that allows you to explore the world in vivid detail. It's not just handy for scouting countries you wish to visit, but also a distracting means of sneaking a peak at neighbours' gardens and the grounds of the rich and famous.

■ The world, as you have never seen it before – in Google Earth

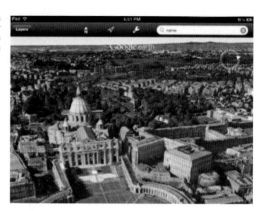

■ Use Wikihood to get a wealth of information on local areas

Travel

Your iPad is the perfect travel companion, especially when packed with our selection of essential Travel apps. There are apps for every stage of your trip. Before you go, use apps to read hotel reviews from fellow travellers before making a hotel booking, or plan which places to visit when abroad by following other's recommendations. Use apps to search for the best travel deals (whether flight or car hire) and make a booking directly from your iPad. If you're planning to travel by plane we have an app to let you check out all the latest flight details. If you're staying at home you can use an app to take a tour of local points of interest and learn about your town's history. There's even an app that turns your iPad 2's camera into a foreign text translator (though it is limited to dealing with short signs that have nice clean fonts). And it all takes up a lot less space than an A-Z and a bumper English/French phrasebook!

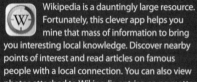

■ Kayak allows you to find cheap hotels and flights easily

■ Read reviews and then find places of interest on a map with Trip Advisor

Utilities

Thanks to the App Store's Utilities category you can turn your iPad into the type of gadget that James Bond would be proud to own (although he'd probably trash it before the end of the movie!). There are Utility apps that enable you to pinpoint your iPad's location on a map and even wipe its precious data if it falls into enemy hands. If your iPad is stolen then there are secure data storage apps that will keep your passwords and bank details safe from prying eyes. If you regularly access websites that use Flash content then there is a web browser that can suit your needs. And there are many more brilliant apps available on the App Store that perform thousands of other cool functions – so make sure you have a browse through them and you're sure to find plenty of apps with a license to thrill.

> ## "There are apps that perform thousands of cool functions"

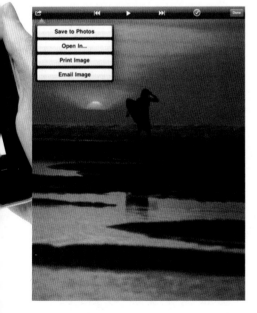

■ Watch Flash content on your iPad with the brilliant Skyfire Web Browser app

■ FileBrowser allows you to transfer files between devices with ease

5 essential apps

01 Find My iPhone
Price: Free **Developer:** Apple

If you only download one app from the Utility category then make sure that it's this one. It could save you lots of time, stress and expense (though you'll need to make sure that the Find My iPad option is turned on in the Settings>iCloudmenu). If you lose your iPad, download the Find My iPhone software onto your Mac or iPhone. It'll pin-point your device's location on a map.

02 1Password Pro
Price: £10.49/$14.99 **Developer:** Agile Web Solutions

If you find it hard to remember multiple passwords then the 1Password Pro app will help. This enables you to store passwords for accounts like bank, MobileMe or iTunes safely. It'll even log you into your password-protected websites with a tap. It may be a relatively pricey app, but if someone gets their hands on your financial data then it could cost you a lot more.

03 Skyfire Web Browser for iPad
Price: £2.99/$4.99 **Developer:** Skyfire Labs, Inc

This web browsing app has always been a popular replacement for Safari and featured tabbed browsing months prior to the iOS 5 release. The best thing about this app is that it is an iPad web browser that actually lets you watch Flash content and has now undergone a few iOS enhancements of its own, including the option to switch to desktop content in an instant.

04 Chrome
Price: Free **Developer:** Google, Inc

Another web browsing app, but you'd do well to remember that Chrome usually boasts the best new features first, and in recent iOS updates, Apple has been playing catch up with its own flagship Safari app – the dual purpose search/address field being a case in point.

05 FileBrowser
Price: £2.99/$4.99 **Developer:** Stratospherix

Having this app installed on your device is akin to having Windows Explorer or Mac Finder on your iPad that allows you to access network folders on Macs, Windows, Linux and NAS drives. You can stream movies and music over Wi-Fi at home, access servers at work and work remotely with confidence that all of your files can be transferred around without any problems. For the price you pay, this is rammed full of features.

Essential apps

■ In this baking-specific version, there are cakes aplenty to get you salivating

Food and drink

Mobile devices have found their way into most areas of our lives, from when we're in the office to watching movies at home, and they are now even helping us out in the kitchen. This explains the addition of a Food and Drink category within the App Store, with the section dealing with all manner of apps for helping you out with food choices, recipe ideas and video tutorials. There are apps aplenty to give you some extra inspiration and indeed encourage you to bring your device into the kitchen. It's not all just eating in however; this section is home to recommendation apps that help you find places to eat out, restaurants and bars based on your location, and apps that aggregate reviews of different venues to help you find exactly what you're looking for.

■ The main tile page of the app is quite stunning to look at and interact with, featuring images of sumptuous recipes to try yourself

■ The app is divided up into various different sections, each bursting with a host of different cocktails to try

■ Each step of a recipe is accompanied by an image of the process in action for a quick-and-easy baking experience

Newsstand

Newsstand has already completely changed the way iOS users consume magazines and newspapers digitally. It makes sense that this part of iOS life now has it's own dedicated area of the App Store, having in the past only been accessible through the native Newsstand app on your device. With an ever-expanding portfolio and the continuing digital revolution that is seeing more publishers releasing digital versions of their magazines and newspapers, Newsstand is well worth spending some time browsing. You can sometimes pick up free issues of certain titles, as well as sign up for free trial periods before committing to a subscription that a lot of the downloads on Newsstand ask for. These are our selections to keep you on top of the news as well as entertained when you want to relax and read on your device.

■ You can easily search the Apple Newsstand section-by-section using the drop-down menu found at the top of the screen

■ Some publications have features that have been redesigned to be interactive for the iPad, for an amazing reading experience

■ Most pages come with their own interactive features

■ There are also plenty of other features on offer, as well as video reports to watch – begin exploring the Newsstand today!

5 essential apps

01 Sport Magazine
Price: Free
Developer: UTV Media

The free weekly sports magazine is available on iOS for nothing, with each issue automatically adding to your library each week. The magazine has been optimised for iPad, with features and articles formatted to look and feel better on the device's screen. The app also allows you to go through back issues from even before you downloaded the app.

02 The Guardian and Observer iPad edition
Price: Free
Developer: Guardian News and Media

With a thirty-day trial for users to test out the app and its content, you can download any article or picture for offline reading and some articles come with image galleries or embedded videos. The interface is impressive, with interactive panels in each section leading to the stories.

03 National Geographic Magazine
Price: £1.99/$2.99
Developer: National Geographic Society

An app that is very image-heavy, Nat Geo requires a subscription. There are video reports as well as interactive maps and the app looks in no way like a magazine – a big part of the appeal. The eye-catching photography makes it well worth the subscription fee.

04 Esquire iPad Edition
Price: Free
Developer: Hearst Communications

One of the best examples of a magazine having made the jump to digital, Esquire uses predominately the exact same content as the print version, but with additional interactive features. Covers can come with videos to show how they were made, and there are pop-up features to flesh out the content.

05 Mad Magazine
Price: Free
Developer: DC Entertainment

This app is excellent value, with a year's subscription available for little more than a single issue of other titles. There isn't a huge amount of extra or interactive content but downloading the app and purchasing a subscription does allow users to view both back issues and current ones.

Your iPad glossary

What does it all mean? We guide you through the common features and terms that you're likely to encounter while using your iPad

APPLE ID
This is the name and password you use to log in to the various Apple services, such as iTunes, the App Store and iCloud.

APPLICATION (APP)
An application, or app, is a software program designed to perform one or more functions. Apps can be downloaded from the App Store.

APP STORE
The App Store is a digital distribution platform for Apple users. Users are able to browse, purchase and download iPad and iPhone apps from the App Store to run on their device.

■ You can shop and browse apps by popularity and category at the App Store

DOCK
The Dock is a row of icons that can be set to appear at the bottom of your Home screen. The Dock is ever-present as you scroll through screens and allows you to access your favourite, most well-used apps easily. You can add and remove apps by pressing and holding on an icon until it starts to shake and then dragging it into position.

GAME CENTER
Apple's gaming portal where you can shop for new games, find friends and play against them online or compare high scores.

GESTURES
These refer to the finger commands that you perform on your iPad's touch screen to carry out various functions. Multitasking Gestures were added to iOS 5 and later, that let you use five fingers to pinch to reveal your Home screen or swipe up, left or right to reveal your multitasking bar or cycle between open apps.

GESTURES JARGON:
● **TAP**
This is the most common and basic gesture to perform on your iPad; it involves tapping the screen with your finger.

● **DOUBLE-TAP**
This involves tapping an object twice in succession. You use this gesture mainly for zooming or highlighting text.

● **TAP, HOLD & DRAG**
Some functions, such as highlighting text, copying and pasting require that you tap and hold down on the screen and then drag your finger to select what you want.

● **PINCH**
To zoom in or to open something, place your thumb and index finger, pinched together, on screen and spread them apart. To zoom out, perform the reverse.

● **SWIPE**
Swiping is one of your primary navigational tools. You perform a left or right swiping motion with your index finger to move through app pages or images in the Photos app, for instance.

HOME BUTTON
This is the large circular button on the front of your iPad that you use to quit apps and return to your iPad's Home screen.

HOME SCREEN
This is essentially the desktop of your iPad that you see when you boot up or unlock your device. From your Home screen you can launch apps and access your Settings.

iCLOUD
The iCloud is a free cloud storage and syncing service available with iOS 5 and iOS 6. With iCloud you can share data, files, music and photographs between devices without the need for manual connecting, syncing and transferring.

iCLOUD JARGON:
● **iTUNES IN THE CLOUD**
With iCloud, the music you purchase from iTunes appears automatically on all of your devices. You can also download past purchases where you want, when you want.

PHOTO STREAM
With iCloud, when you take a photo on one device, it automatically appears on all of your devices. Photos transferred from a digital camera connected to your Mac will also be pushed to your mobile devices.

DOCUMENTS IN THE CLOUD
If you have the same iCloud-enabled apps on more than one device, iCloud automatically keeps your documents up to date across all devices.

iOS
Whereas Macs run on an operating system called OS X, your mobile devices – iPhone, iPad and iPod touch – use iOS. The latest version is iOS 6 and you will need this installed in order to enjoy the benefits of iCloud.

iTUNES
This is Apple's flagship digital distribution centre that lets users browse, purchase and download a wide range of digital media, including music, books, movies and TV shows. Using an Apple ID, users log in and store payment details to make downloading media quick and easy.

iTUNES JARGON:
FEATURED
All of the latest, most notable music, movies and TV shows will be showcased under this tab at the front of their respective store windows.

TOP CHARTS
See what's hot and popular on the iTunes Store by tapping on this tab.

■ iTunes is the ultimate digital marketplace for buying and downloading new music and entertainment through your iPad

GENIUS
This is a feature that recommends new music, films and shows based on what is currently in your library. Genius can also create playlists for you.

iTUNES U
iTunes is also a great source of educational materials, and you'll find a wide range of digital books, videos and podcasts by clicking on the 'iTunes U' link.

REDEEM
Occasionally you may be gifted a product from iTunes in the form of a code. Click on the 'Redeem' link and input the code to download the product.

NEWSSTAND
This app comes free with iOS 5 and iOS 6 and is a place where all of your digital magazines and newspapers are stored and can be accessed.

SAFARI
This is Apple's premier web browsing app that comes as standard with all iPad operating systems. The app boasts a wealth of new iOS 6 enhancements to make surfing the web a quick and easy experience.

SETTINGS
Accessible from the Dock or Home Screen, Settings is where you can tweak all aspects of your iPad and the apps and utilities that make it tick.

SIDE SWITCH
This is the small switch on the edge of the iPad that you can assign, via Settings, to act as a mute button or to lock your screen rotation.

SLEEP/WAKE BUTTON
This is the lozenge-shaped button on top of the iPad that you use to turn your device on and off.

WI-FI
Wi-Fi refers to a wireless networking system that allows you to connect to the internet without any cables. You will need access to a wireless router for this to work with your iPad.

■ The Newsstand app is where all of your digital magazines and newspapers are safely stored

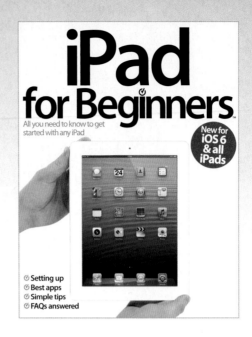

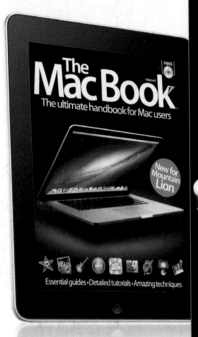
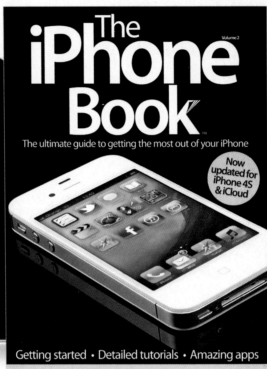